JONATHAN EDWARDS,
The Valley and Nature

Other books by Clyde A. Holbrook:

Faith and Community

Religion, A Humanistic Field

Jonathan Edwards's Original Sin (editor)

The Ethics of Jonathan Edwards

The Iconoclastic Deity

JONATHAN EDWARDS,
The Valley and Nature

An Interpretative Essay

Clyde A. Holbrook

LEWISBURG
BUCKNELL UNIVERSITY PRESS
LONDON AND TORONTO: ASSOCIATED UNIVERSITY PRESSES

Associated University Presses
440 Forsgate Drive
Cranbury, NJ 08512

Associated University Presses
25 Sicilian Avenue
London WC1A 2QH, England

Associated University Presses
2133 Royal Windsor Drive
Unit 1
Mississauga, Ontario
Canada L5J 1K5

The paper used in this publication meets the requirements
of the American National Standard for Permanence of Paper
for Printed Library Materials Z39.48-1984.

Library of Congress Cataloging-in-Publication Data

Holbrook, Clyde A.
  Jonathan Edwards, the valley and nature.

  Bibliography: p.
  Includes index.
  1. Edwards, Jonathan, 1703–1758. I. Title.
BX7260.E3H58   1987   230'.58'0924   86-47915
ISBN 0-8387-5117-2 (alk. paper)

Printed in the United States of America

Contents

If existence is more worthy than defect and nonentity, and if any created existence is in itself worthy to be, then this knowledge of God and his glory is worthy to be. The existence of the created universe consists as much in it as in anything, yea, it is one of the highest, most real and substantial parts of all created existence; most remote from nonentity and defect.

—Miscellany 1225 (ca. 1752)

When we survey nature and think however flitting and superficial has been the animal enjoyment of its wonders, and when we realize how incapable the separate cells and pulsations of each flower are of enjoying the total effect—then our sense of the values of the detail for the totality dawns upon our consciousness. This is the intuition of holiness, the intuition of the sacred, which is at the foundation of all religion.

—Whitehead, *Modes of Thought*

Preface

Many books and articles have been written on Jonathan Edwards, and probably no one of them does justice to the multifaceted nature of the man and his thought. This work can look for no better prospect. However, my own interest in him, unlike that of some scholars, arose from my acquaintance with the scene in which much of his life was lived, and where he carried on much of his most important thinking. The explanation of this circumstance is amplified in the introduction below, and although it was not determinative of the turn that my interpretation of Edwards's ideas took, it added for me a certain personal quality that I have not discovered in other writers on Edwards.

I wish to acknowledge my gratitude to the Yale University Press for permission to quote from *The Works of Jonathan Edwards*, vol. 6, Wallace E. Anderson, editor, and to the Beinecke Rare Book and Manuscript Library of Yale University for permission to cite several passages from its manuscripts of Jonathan Edwards's "Miscellanies." I am also grateful to Ruth Mastin Anderson for permission to cite from her late husband's work on "Notes on Typology." Professor Thomas A. Schafer, to whom all Edwards scholars are indebted, has graciously allowed me to refer to a number of his transcriptions of Edwards's "Miscellanies." The substance of chapters 1, 2, and 5 was delivered as the Mead-Swing lectures at Oberlin College in October 1986.

I dedicate the book to my wife, Dorothy, who has managed to make sense of my scribbles and has typed the manuscript. She has lived with Edwards quite as long as I have.

Prologue

In 1754 Jonathan Edwards, perhaps for the last time, returned to the Connecticut Valley. He had left it a tarnished figure, having been cast out of his church in Northampton in 1750. The following year he had settled in a frontier church and mission in Stockbridge. From there he had come to the little settlement known as Green River, now known as Greenfield. It must have been a long, tedious, and arduous journey from the Berkshire hills to this little settlement. I know neither the route he took nor what hospitality he enjoyed along the way, but he had a cause to serve, and the many miles did not deter him from it. He came to Greenfield to preside over a church council that was to decide upon the installation of one Reverend Edward Billings as the pastor of a church that Edwards himself had earlier helped to establish.

Once more he was to be involved in an ecclesiastical quarrel. In 1753 a council had been held that refused to install Billings. He had been dismissed from his parish in Belchertown, then called Cold Spring, partly because of his support of Edwards at the council that recommended Edwards's dismissal. The first council at Greenfield had been dominated by the Reverend Jonathan Ashley and his supporters from Deerfield. It was Ashley who had helped to sever Edwards from his Northampton parish. Understandably, Ashley would not want a pastor in the vicinity who clung to Edwards's theological views and ecclesiastical practices. Consequently, Billings was denied installation. Now, the second time around, Edwards himself had come to cast his considerable weight on the side of the unfortunate candidate. This time no representatives from Deerfield appeared, and with Edwards's help Billings was to be installed. Edwards was repaying Billings for his earlier support. Edwards would have had to be a saint if he did not relish, in a roundabout fashion, revenge for Ashley's earlier opposition to himself.[1]

This minor episode scarcely warrants more than a footnote in

Edwards's career, but it strikes a chord in my own life, since I was born in Greenfield and lived there until I went to college. In the seventeenth century what was to become Greenfield was a scarcely settled tract of land abutting Deerfield on the north. Only after a bitter struggle with Deerfield over boundaries was this land set off as a separate district. On 9 June 1753 the town of Greenfield was incorporated. Its territory extended to the Connecticut River on the East. It was therefore one of the small villages that from the seventeenth century on dotted the Valley from Connecticut to the Hampshire Grants. South of Greenfield lay Deerfield, Whately, Hatfield, Hadley, and to the southeast, Sunderland. Farther south in Massachusetts lay Northampton and Springfield, which by the eighteenth century had become virtual metropolises. These towns were the western and northwestern frontiers of Massachusetts, and they had borne the brunt of French and Indian attacks. However, when Edwards, after his grandfather's death, assumed the pastorate in Northampton, warfare in that area had largely ceased.

In the heyday of the religious awakenings Edwards was a well-known figure in all these towns. He never wielded the political and spiritual authority of his maternal grandfather, Solomon Stoddard, but he was nevertheless an imposing force in the religious life of the Valley. During his pastorate he occasionally preached in towns outside the Valley, but in the main his career was bounded by it. His cultural and spiritual roots were planted and nourished there, and it was there that those first impressions of nature, which were so deeply to affect his thought, were formed, first in his boyhood at East Windsor and later by experiences at Northampton. "No wonder the beauty and majesty of nature stamped themselves unforgettably on his early thought," wrote Ola Winslow.[2]

The reader will, I hope, forgive my historical romanticism stirred by so small a thing as learning that Edwards, long before my time, had visited my town. As a boy and youth I had probably heard of Jonathan Edwards, but I am sure I would have cared little and known less about him. As I later learned, he was not the sort of person to whom a lad of my upbringing would have been attracted. Furthermore, although I was brought up in close relation to my church, I cannot say that my intellectual interest in matters religious was very keen. My idea of a minister was certainly not one that included the Edwards of popular imagination. But there have been two factors in my youthful experiences that were destined to draw me to the study of Edwards. From an early age I had a consuming interest in local colonial history. I lived only three miles from Deerfield, which had been sacked by the French and Indians in 1704. Arrowheads were still being plowed up in my day. The knob of a hill where the attacking party spent the night before the raid still humps up north of the town. Stories were told; houses remain that survived the attack; names of families whose ancestors were part of that history are still current in the vicinity. All these early impressions and many more have been interwoven into a tapestry of memories that bind me to a locale that will ever be of more than sentimental value. Into that repository of historical memory Jonathan Edwards was to fit comfortably, adding an aspect that enriched what already lay in the background of my mind. My sense of history was scarcely second to my love of the countryside. When, thanks to Ricarda Clark of Oberlin, I came upon the episode of Edwards's coming to Greenfield, I thought—because of my historical sense, I suppose—I have walked or ridden over the same landscape as he did, not only in my home town but in other places in the Valley. He viewed the hills to the west of Greenfield rising to the Berkshires. He traveled up and down the Valley and saw the fertile meadows around Deerfield, Sunderland, and those other river towns. Mount Tom, whose height, tradition tells us, he attempted to measure, looms near Northampton, and the jumbled Mount Holyoke range running off to the east was there when he was in the Valley. This was the land whose serene beauty I drank in, as I believe Edwards did also. It left an impression upon me that even my experience of the majestic heights of the Rockies has never effaced. It was home to me, as it was for Edwards. I saw it for what it was, but unlike Edwards I never gave thought to fashioning religious truths from its contours or its flora and fauna. Yet it was this nature that moved Edwards to some of his most eloquent prose.

This combination of historical memory and love of nature on my part came together in my study of Edwards. I have come to believe that nature contributed far more to Edwards's philosophy, theology, and ethics than has usually been allowed by his interpreters. I find myself, therefore, at odds with the opinion of one author, who has argued that Edwards's principal purpose in his published works was "to set nature apart from supernature in the domain of religious experience."[3] In what follows I do not deny that Edwards was a God-intoxicated thinker, nor that the spiritual life was the essence of his life and thought, but I shall endeavor to show that to a high degree the realm by which he adumbrated the spiritual life was that of nature as directly experienced, and philosophically and scientifically interpreted. This book is a thought experiment, as Kierkegaard would have said, in following out that theme. In one sense I am saying that Edwards never completely left the Valley. In another sense he soared above its confines by his metaphysical and religious insights.

JONATHAN EDWARDS,
The Valley and Nature

1

The Valley and Nature at First Hand

THROUGH geological ages the Connecticut River from its source above Beecher Falls in present New Hampshire carved a spacious valley extending through Massachusetts and Connecticut, at last pouring its waters into Long Island Sound near Old Saybrook, Connecticut. It left extensive fertile plains suitable for agriculture and hunting, and in its lower reaches provided a handy means of travel and commerce. Hills guided its course to frame a pleasant scenic contrast to the open lands they bordered.

As unlikely as it may seem, the presence of hills and mountains once gave rise to theological debates concerning whether or not the earth had degenerated since the Creation. Henry More, one of Edwards's admired authors, opined in 1653 that mountains might seem but "so many wens and unnatural protuberances upon the face of the earth," but he reflected that without them there would be no rivers. They were therefore useful. In 1681 Thomas Burnet claimed that the earth had originally been as smooth as an egg until it was broken up and "deformed" by the Deluge after man sinned. His opponents denied with a straight face that the earth was imperfect and claimed that mountains were indispensable in creating rivers, providing natural frontiers, and providing "a congenial home for goats."[1] Whether Edwards was aware of this geotheological controversy we do not know, but he offered his own theories concerning the relation of mountains, valleys, and rivers. The uneven, confused hills and mountains and their valleys seemed to him to be without design, casually dispersed over the face of the earth. Yet together they constituted convenient channels for water to reach the ocean. When the world was created, he thought, it was covered by water. The earth, being soft and loose, was worn and altered by the motion of the waters. However, he had to assume that there were varying degrees of hardness and softness in the earth to explain how some places left by the water

15

were higher than others. The softest portion of the earth gave way to the waters and became channels for the receding water. After the waters had gone, these channels remained to carry off the water "afterwards gushing out in various parts of the continent." The process recurred after the Flood, leaving the earth as now seen with its mountains, valleys, and rivers.

This geological theory Edwards put to use to explain the Connecticut River itself. Large rivers have what he called "campaign countries without stones" along their borders, and are flanked by ridges of mountains running roughly parallel to them. Closer to the river there are meadows, lower than the plain, and last of all the channel itself "as here in the Connecticut River."[2] So the Connecticut Valley had been formed, and within its embrace Edwards was born, grew up, and lived most of his life.

In passing, though the matter is not unimportant, it should be noted that his reflections on the geological creation of the Valley were discriminatingly realistic without a hint of that form of philosophical idealism which made of nature a system of sensations and ideas. It was physical nature, as such, with which he dealt. Neither was there any reference in this passage to a symbolism or typology that would derogate from the independent reality of what he was describing and about which he was theorizing. The metaphysical and typological interpretations of the creation and behavior of rivers were to be found elsewhere in his writings. In them he would liken rivers to the Providence of God that is consummated in God himself, as are rivers that at last flow into the sea from which they come.[3]

Today the contours of the land remain as Edwards saw them, but the river no longer pursues its way unhampered by human artifices. In many places its power has been dammed for the energy demanded by a modern industrial society. Cities like Holyoke, Chicopee, Springfield, and Hartford spread their manufacturing interests along its banks, often marring its pristine beauty. Northampton, a college city, is no longer the village Edwards knew. Now it is cluttered with the signs of urban living. Yet the foothills of the Berkshires mount guard west of the river and eastward loom the Mount Holyoke range's disheveled heights. Mount Tom still lifts its head, while farther to the north Sugar Loaf abruptly breaks the plain to overlook the fields of Sunderland. At Greenfield the Mohawk Trail, no longer following closely the path once trod by raiding Indian warriors, begins its climb toward eastern New York State. The Northfields lie to the north, where once stood a fort to withstand marauding Indians. So the towns and cities change, but the land knows only the slow, imperceptible erosion of geological and climatic changes. Of much of the Valley's history and scenery the modern driver, speeding along present-day Interstate 91, may be unaware or indifferent, but its tranquil conformations remain to delight the eye of those like Edwards in yesteryear who take the time to appreciate them.

Shorn of its modern attractions and defilements, the Valley was the setting for Edward's life, and the stimulus of his imagination and thought. Born on his father's farm in East Windsor, Connecticut, he grew up in rural surroundings where life hovered close to the elements of earth and sky. Yet I cannot think of him as sharing in the everyday tasks of plowing or animal husbandry as a farmer's son should do. His father, the village pastor, tutored young lads for Harvard or Yale, and oversaw young Jonathan's early education, ably assisted by his remarkable wife. So prepared in 1716, Jonathan went off to Yale College, sometimes located at Wethersfield, later at New Haven, where he remained until 1722. After a brief pastorate in New York City, 1722–23, he returned to Yale to serve as tutor under great difficulties, while he pursued further studies from 1724 to 1726. Then he came to Northampton as assistant to his maternal grandfather, Solomon Stoddard, whom he succeeded as pastor in 1729. There he remained until 1750, when under a cloud of dissension and strife, for which he was in part responsible, he was dismissed, a virtual outcast from the town and the clerical profession. A year later he left the Valley, to return for the last time, as far as we know, for the church council held in Greenfield. He had accepted the thankless jobs of being a minister to a small English-speaking parish and acting as missionary to the Indians gathered at the frontier settlement of Stockbridge. At that post, in spite of ill health, of controversies concerning the administration of the mission, and of frequent exposure to the dangers of Indian assault, he completed some of his most important treatises. In 1757 he reluctantly accepted the call of the presidency of a fledgling institution in New Jersey, later to become Princeton University, where he died of a smallpox inoculation in 1758.

Edwards had traveled to Boston occasionally, and during the Great Awakening had preached in several New England towns outside the Valley, but he had never traveled to a foreign country or lived in a cosmopolitan center. His brief stays at New York City, Stockbridge, and Princeton were scarcely more than interruptions in his Valley experiences. To all outward appearances his career was carried on in geographical, cultural, and intellectual isolation. Yet, in deep communion with nature, his Bible, and God, with his mind stimulated by books bought and borrowed and by correspondence with acquaintances abroad, he fed upon insights that breached his geographical and cultural confines. To an extraordinary degree he surmounted, intellectually and spiritually, the limitations of his time and place, although his mature thought was often to show the price exacted by isolation.

During the seventeenth century, settlement of the Connecticut Valley did not always enjoy support from ecclesiastical and political authorities in Boston. When the Reverened Thomas Hooker and his congregation betook themselves to the Valley in present-day Connecticut, they did so in the face of criticisms and warnings as to what would befall them in the wilderness. Their venture removed them both physically and spiritually from the society of eastern Massachusetts, where it was supposed that the ideal form of church-state relations was practiced. But now the move to what could then be accounted western lands was an invitation to loosen the whole organic skein of religious, ethical, and social bonds that should properly mark a truly Christian community. Neglect of family order and worship could be expected, increased resistance of individuals to authority would occur, and civilized behavior might be sloughed off by association with wild Indian manners and customs. The frontier wilderness was in more than one sense a dangerous place, and there were those in positions of authority in and about Boston who darkly prophesied that no good would come from such ventures into the wilderness.

Both in fact and fantasy, the word *wilderness* played an important role in Puritan thought. Generally it referred to any uncivilized area, the wilder the more dangerous, where Satan and his minions—often identified as Indian savages—perpetrated all manner of evil in opposition to God's kingdom and his faithful subjects. *Wilderness* also referred to whatever was uncouth, tumultuous, unregulated by convention, good sense, or law. It was a term that could be used as an appropriate image of life in the world outside the church. So Roger Williams claimed, "The Wildernesse is a cleer resemblance of the world, heer greedie and furious men persecute and devoure the harmless and innocent as the wilde beasts pursue the Hinds and Roes."[4] To live in an actual wilderness where beasts of prey prowled and sinister spiritual powers held sway was enough to daunt the hardiest soul. And what Cotton Mather called a "wilderness condition" could call down upon the heads of innocent people "crop failures, sea disasters, droughts and every ill" to which New England flesh was heir.[5]

In spite of dire warnings concerning the perils of wilderness living, people from eastern Massachusetts and southern Connecticut settled up and down the Valley. In the late seventeenth and early eighteenth centuries it became an inland frontier whose residents often endured the brutality of the seemingly interminable warfare between France and England. Its small villages like Deerfield, Hadley, and Northfield paid dearly in loss of property, life, and freedom as protective buffers for the coastal towns of New England. But people came to their land often less prompted by reasons of shoring up England's military cause than to seek economic fortune and to extend Christian faith and civilization into lands reckoned to be spiritually barren and open to exploitation. The hope was held that the "noxious weeds of the wilderness could be rooted out and the land improved to flower as a garden."[6] The word *wilderness* itself underwent a change in meaning as settlers penetrated to the Valley. What greeted their eyes was not a *wilderness*, if by that term one meant to describe a land filled with brambles, trees, and forbidding rocky soil. Before them lay a pleasant, fertile valley to be used. Northampton and Springfield became trading posts, while farmers set about taming a wilderness that bore little resemblance to their visions of a desolate terrain. It was a wilderness only in the sense that Christian faith and civilization had not yet been established there.

When Northampton was founded in 1653, those seeking its establishment cited as reasons to the General court of Massachusetts the advantage of further enlarging the territories of the Gospel and the securing of a comfortable subsistence. Later in 1665 when Royal Commissioners threatened its charter and liberties, the town justified its position by arguing that the Lord had there transformed New England from "a wilderness to a fruitful field."[7] So when Edwards came there in the fall of 1726, it could scarcely be called a town set down in a wilderness. It was by that time relatively free from attack, and its inhabitants could work their fields without fear. But this outward security did little to abate their incessant squabbling over boundaries and the possession of valuable lands—quarrels that had been going on even under the ministry of Solomon Stoddard.[8] Edwards inherited this wrangling, unfortunately, and it helped to exacerbate the troubles that led to his dismissal. In spite of the settled appearance of the town, the word *wilderness* maintained its pejorative power in theological jargon. So in reckoning the manner in which revivals operated, Edwards laid hold upon the word. "When God is about to turn the earth into a paradise," he wrote, "he don't begin his work where there is some good growth already, but in a wilderness, where nothing grows, and nothing is to be seen but dry sand and barren rocks. . . ."[9] Of course, he was speaking of a spiritual wilderness that owed its features more to biblical landscapes than it did to the view from his study window.

However, to speak of a valley is also to speak of mountains and hills, forests and thickets—in short, a wilderness round about a valley. When Sereno Dwight sketched the features of the several environments where his famous ancestor was born and lived, the wilderness theme sounded in counterpoint to the note of civilization. The place of Edward's birth he described as "delightfully situated in the valley of the Connecticut . . . distinguished for the fertility of its soil, and the beauty of its scenery." On the other hand, he called East Windsor "an obscure colony in the midst of a wilderness," and he wrote off Northampton as a frontier village, and Stockbridge as a "still humbler hamlet."[10] The better to set off the genius of Edwards against the background of cultural isolation, Dwight identified his birthplace as one where "the ancient reign of barbarism was only beginning to yield to the inroads of culture and civilization," an area sparsely settled, surrounded by a vast continuous forest. The site was "distant three thousand miles from Europe, the seat of arts, refinement and knowledge." Northampton was "in the very frontier," while at Stockbridge Edwards lived "in the midst of savage life."[11] In spite of these bleak assessments of Edwards's natural and cultural surroundings, Dwight went as far as to describe Northampton as "uncommonly pleasant" and possessed of "more than the ordinary share of refinement and polish."[12] Thus the interplay of wilderness and Valley, wilderness and culture, was described. Edwards was positioned both physically and culturally between the two, with plenty of opportunity to react to each.

Edwards himself left us descriptions of Northampton and its inhabitants. The people were "as sober, and orderly, and good sort" as any in New England. Seldom if ever had he known "as rational and understanding a people." The town, he felt, had been remarkably free from religious error, sectarian opinions, and ecclesiastical quarrels. It had been spared the ravages of moral evil because vice had not penetrated that far into the hinterland; "our being so far within the land, at a distance from seaports, and in a corner of the country" helped to explain this fortunate condition. Since that part of the valley was "much separated from other parts of the province," it had comparatively little intercourse with them, a fact that allowed the people to manage their ecclesiastical affairs in isolation from distractions in other parts of New England.[13] However, he also pointed out that after some early religious awakenings and the death of Stoddard the town experienced a period of dullness in religion, a failure of family discipline, and contention between two groups in the town.

These generally optimistic estimates were penned before the debacle of his dismissal as pastor. Later, in a letter to Thomas Gillespie, written from Stockbridge, a very different picture was painted of the people and circumstances of Northampton. "The people of North-ampton," he wrote bitterly, "are not the most happy in their tem-pers." Ever since he could remember, they had been high-spirited, stiff-necked, and of a turbulent temper. Party spirit in the town had rent the church and risen to such a point of hostility that "a member of one party met the head of the opposite party, and assaulted him and beat him unmercifully." With the growth of wealth in the town and the spread of its reputation for religious virtues, its people had succumbed to spiritual pride, setting them beyond "the reach of all rule and instruction."[14] However, these were the words of a man whose career was in virtual ruins, one who had fallen prey to the machinations of his enemies and been left adrift as a dishonored figure.

Edwards's description of the isolation of Northampton was not entirely accurate. True, it was not within easy distance of villages to the east, and a trip to Boston was not one to be lightly undertaken. And to the west stood the barrier of the Berkshires before one came to the Hudson Valley. Yet the towns to the north and south enjoyed ease of access to each other because of the configuration of the Connecticut Valley. Travel and commerce followed the river. So when the early revivals began, their range at first scarcely extended beyond the valley.[15] Its bounds framed a community of sorts, compounded of social, economic, and religious interests. Thus Northampton was not isolated except as part of a larger reach of territory that was isolated.

The isolation of Stockbridge was a different matter. It was a settle-ment on the road to nowhere, isolated in the wilderness of western Massachusetts. There the word *wilderness* in its full physical and cultural meaning could be felt. For the benefit of his Scottish corre-spondent, Mr. McCullough, Edwards described his situation as one "about 40 miles west of the Connecticut River, about 25 miles east of Hudson's river, and about 35 miles east from Albany; a place exposed in this time of war."[16] The words attached to a map of the period gave an even more depressing account of the location of Stockbridge. It was positioned within "a wilderness of forty miles on the east, a wood of twenty miles on the west, and a great and terrible wilderness on the north of several hundred miles in extent which reached to Can-ada." Ephraim Williams told of the difficulties of communication with the outside world in his letters to his son, then at the College of New Jersey (Princeton). His letters from Stockbridge usually had to be carried through the forest to the Hudson River, where one Captain Fonda delivered them by boat to New York, where they were picked up as opportunity allowed by a "Mr. Burke at Whitehall."[17] Under such circumstances it is remarkable that Edwards managed to carry on a brisk correspondence with friends on both sides of the Atlantic. Harassed by the same Williams family that had helped to hound him from his Northampton pulpit, subject to recurrent illness, and fearful of attacks from unfriendly Indians, Edwards probably had neither the time nor the inclination to revel in the beauties of nature, as he had had in the Valley.

The earliest intimations of the part nature played in Edwards's life and thought are customarily found in his "Personal Narrative." This is a piece to be approached with some care. The development of Edwards's religious life shown in it was written in retrospect, and therefore is colored deeply by ideas developed long after the events and descriptions of his spiritual estate occurred. The reader cannot be confident that what is before him is the earliest evidence of first-hand experience; rather, as in much autobiographical writing, the experience is so overlaid with didactic purpose and matured thought that one must look beyond the words themselves. How far, for example, was his deprecation of his boyhood religious experiences affected by his later experience of those who claimed to be wrought upon by the Spirit, only to fall away after the revival spirit waned? How could he count his boyish religious exercises as "self-righteous pleasure," except by reflection on the pride of those whose affections proved false? Was his twofold conversion to the doctrine of divine sovereignty a way of making clear to his readers that intellectual conviction, in which he detected no "extraordinary influence of God's Spirit in it" but only assurance of its justice and reasonableness, was to be distinguished from the later delightful conviction, when presumably a new sense and appreciation of divine sovereignty filled his soul? Had he read back into this crucial event the distinction between speculative knowledge and heartfelt conviction that he later developed? As David C. Pierce observed, Edwards's interest in nature "so fresh and uninhibited in the Narrative, was largely emptied of its concrete significance in Edwards' later attempts to emblemize the old story of sin and grace."[18]

We may not be able satisfactorily to answer these questions, but the fact that he was from his early years much affected by nature in connection with his religious feelings cannot be doubted. As a lad, with his schoolmates, he built a "booth in a swamp, in a very retired spot," and he retired to other secret places in the woods by himself for religious exercises.[19] The new apprehensions of God and Christ that descended upon him after coming to terms with divine sovereignty led him to a kind of vision "of being alone in the mountains or some solitary wilderness" as he grew older. Having talked with his father of his experiences, he told of walking by himself "in a solitary place in my father's pasture." As his sense of divine things increased and grew more lively, "the appearance of everything was altered." God's excellence, wisdom, purity, and love appeared in everything about him, "in the sun, moon and stars; in the clouds and blue sky; in the grass, flowers, trees; in the water and all nature. . . ." Even the thunder and lightning that once had frightened him became part of his sweet contemplation, so that with the approach of a storm he positioned himself "in order to view the clouds and see the lightnings play and hear the majestic and awful voice of God's thunder. . . ."[20]

In New York later he followed his custom of solitary meditation and converse with nature by visiting the banks of the Hudson. And on the way home from New York he stopped at Saybrook where, he said, "I had a sweet and refreshing season, walking alone in the fields."[21] In his diary he recorded his memories of New York. "I used to conceive myself as walking in the fields at home; but now I am at home I conceive myself as walking in the fields I used to frequent at New York." He recalled the meditations he had had at Westchester, and those he had enjoyed "in the orchard and those under the oak-tree."[22]

As pastor in Northampton, he told of riding out into the woods for his health, and having found a retired place, he would fall into meditation and prayer.[23] In Sarah Pierrepont, his wife-to-be, he found one with a similar attraction to nature as a place for contemplation. Of her he wrote, "She loves to be alone, walking in fields and groves."[24] And he marked as one of the signs of deep religious affections that "true religion disposes persons to be much alone, in solitary places, for holy meditation and prayer."[25] Indeed, in a peculiar sense one might take as an earmark of Edwards's character and career the phrase *to be much alone in solitary places*—places where the brooding silence or overwhelming power of God and nature ministered to his devotional life as did his study to his intellectual life.

Yet this predilection for meditation in the solitude of nature is less striking when viewed against the background of a similar tendency common in Britain in the same period. Edwards was by no means unique in the measure of his sensitivity to the impact of nature upon the religious life. The same Francis Hutcheson whom he gently criticized in *The Nature of True Virtue* wrote in 1725, "The beauty of trees, their cool shades, and their aptness to conceal from observation, have made groves and woods the usual retreat to those who love solitude." The poet Henry Needler found that among trees "my thoughts naturally take a solemn and religious turn," and Bulstrode Whitelocke referred to Saint Francis to support his opinion that "every leaf, plant and briar was a book of God, declaring his power and goodness."

Vicenius Knox felt the power of trees so alluring that he pitied a man who could not fall in love with a tree.[26] These people may not have shared Edwards's "delightful conviction" of divine sovereignty. One did not have to possess that divine and supernatural sense Edwards prized to find God amid groves and woods. On the other hand, Edwards probably never would have embraced Knox's idea of falling in love with a tree. Instead, at one place he flatly stated that "the body of man is no more capable of being the subject of love or hatred . . . than the body of a tree. . . ." Yet he admitted that "there is that which is peculiarly wonderful in trees, beyond anything that is in the inanimate world."[27] And he took it as a sign of the work of grace in Abigail Hutchinson that she had grown extremely sensitive to God's glory "appearing in the trees and growth of the fields."[28]

It is worthy of comment that Edwards's deepest experiences of God as described in his "Personal Narrative" and "Diary" did not occur with Bible in hand or in a church. He was undoubtedly in a high state of religious excitement in these experiences, but he did not lose his grip upon the sheer facticity of nature. He did not treat nature as though it were only an idea in his mind in keeping with the idealism we find elsewhere in his writings. Even there he could affirm "things are what they seem to be."[29] Otherworldly Edwards certainly was in many respects, but as Robert Daly said of Puritan poetry, "the world's body, the physical world sensorily perceived" in poetry, "though not divorced from considerations of that other world," showed undisguised appreciation of this one.[30] To this judgment Edwards was no exception. The fact that nature's beauties suggested spiritual ideas did not erase from his mind the conviction that these ideas were inherent in the details he saw before him. When he rhapsodized over the soul as "a field or garden of God with all manner of pleasant flowers" he followed through his conception by correlating it with "a little white flower." It was "low and humble in the ground, opening its bosom, to receive the pleasant beams of the sun's glory; rejoicing, as it were, in a calm rapture; diffusing around a sweet fragrancy."[31] In this there is as much attention to the flower itself as to the graces it represented. He did not have to betake himself into a different sphere of consciousness to appreciate that such graces inhered in nature itself as God's creation. Certainly Edwards was not unique in finding God's handiwork, power, wisdom, and gracious attributes in nature.[32]

Wallace E. Anderson has suggested that there was little evidence that as a child Edwards had either an interest in or a highly developed skill for minutely observing the phenomena of nature.[33] Edwards's observations on spiders seem to be an exception to this comment, but whether these were simply early scientific efforts or examples of the way in which living creatures aroused his sense of God's presence in nature is probably now unanswerable. The writings themselves may count either way. At least, we find Edwards in first-hand contact with living nature when he wrote "Of Insects." Led by Dwight, some commentators of an earlier period thought these documents showed Edwards to be a promising scientist engaged in critical investigations of nature. In the field of natural philosophy Edwards "might easily have gained its highest honors," thought Dwight. "Had his life been devoted to these pursuits, in a country where he could at once have availed himself of the discoveries of others, and the necessary instruments, he would have met with no ordinary success, in extending the bounds of Physical Science."[34] In large part Dwight based these high expectations on the mistaken belief that Edwards's descriptions of the spider were penned while he was a mere lad. Unfortunately for this opinion, modern research has established the fact that Edwards wrote these pieces later than his biographer assumed, probably in the summer and autumn of 1719, and during a similar period of 1720 after having attended Yale College.[35] Furthermore, Dwight's opinion of Edwards's scientific promise did not reckon sufficiently with Edwards's lack of the mathematical tools to carry on or substantiate the findings of Newton, Boyle, and other scientists. In advice addressed to himself as he set out to write a major treatise, never to be completed, Edwards wrote, "Always, when I have occasion to make use of mathematical proof, to acknowledge my ignorance in mathematics," and he left it to mathematicians to determine whether his remarks were of the nature of mathematical proofs.[36] Later Edwards offered a similar opinion of his mathematical skills as one reason for his reluctance to accept the presidency of the college at Princeton. He admitted to the trustees of that institution that he was deficient in "algebra and the higher parts of mathematics."[37] Fortunately, however, this capability was unnecessary for writing about spiders. All that was needed was careful observation, with but little of what might be called scientific experimentation.

"Of all insects," he proclaimed, "no one is more wonderful than the spider—especially in respect to their sagacity and admirable way of working." Their webs glistening in the sun were "still more wonderful . . . and of such a height as that one would think they were tacked to the sky by one end, were it not they were moving and floating."[38] To explain that spiders appeared to swim in the air Edwards proposed several theories, concluding that nature did things as well or better than we "can imagine beforehand." Thus was exhibited the exuberant goodness of the Creator who provided for all necessities, including the pleasure and recreation of all sort of creatures, even those most despicable.[39] He marked that in warm weather flying insects fly about, only "for their ease and comfort, going in whatever direction the wind blows." Their enjoyment bestows upon them a carefree freedom that suggests an almost lively human character. Yet there is an orderliness to God's creation to be seen in the "wonderful contrivance of annually carrying off and burying the corrupting nauseousness of our air, of which flying insects are little collections, in the bottom of the ocean where it will do no harm. . . ." Thus an ever-multiplying nature, under God's direction, was adjusted and balanced "nicely and mathematically." In spite of this derogatory comment concerning insects, he would write in the "Spider Letter" that everything about them was admirable and wonderful.[40] The sense of wonder that suffused his writings on these creatures in no way blotted out their sensible reality.

The time would come when, in his sermon on Sinners in the Hands of an Angry God, the spider would become the representative of sinful humanity. When Edwards told his rapt congregation that God held each of them over the pit of hell "such as one holds a spider, or some loathsome insect over the fire . . . ," he was no longer praising spiders for their admirable characteristics. Wonder at and pleasure in God's creation had given way to remembrances of "their corrupting nauseousness." Their low status in the economy of nature made them fit symbols for sinners.

Spiders may have lost all charm in Edwards's eyes by the time he gave the sermon, but across the Atlantic these and other lowly creatures had for some time been eliciting such delicacy of feeling that there was opposition to the thoughtless killing of them. According to Keith Thomas, the seventeenth and eighteenth centuries championed the cause of worms, beetles, snails, earwigs, and spiders.[41] In 1653 John Bulwer struck the familiar chord of the "great chain of being" when he warned that by killing toads and spiders "one link of God's chain, one note of harmony" would be lost.[42] By the nineteenth century these sentiments seem to have lost favor. It was then thought by some that birds served a good purpose by snapping up insects, thereby reducing their population. A balance in nature was more desirable than an overstaffing of each level of the "chain of being." As one bit of folk wisdom ran, "If it were not for the Robbin Riddick and the Cutty-Wren, a spider would overcome a man."[43] With that opinion Edwards would have agreed. For him the wind and a heavy atmosphere, as well as birds, restrained insects' fertility by "adjusting their destruction to their multiplication" so that there would always be "just an equal number of them" from year to year.[44] By observation Edwards dealt directly with spiders, but with other forms of life below the human level he dealt less freely and more theoretically. So seldom did he speak admiringly of the brute creation, as he had spoken of spiders, that I suspect that as a boy he never had a dog, calf, or cat as a pet. Yet, in his uncompleted projected treatise he had planned to discuss, along with the propagation and growth of plants, the respiration and blood circulation of animals.[45] In "The Mind," however, he did make observations about animal life, although in these remarks the sense of wonder he had earlier expressed about spiders was lacking. In contrast to man, he affirmed, there was no necessity for supposing animals to be possessed of reason. In this connection Edwards may have had in mind those abroad who believed that animals were endowed with higher sensibilities. Two authors he often quoted on theological subjects held opinions different from his on the brute creation.

Philip Doddridge did not attribute reason to brutes, but he was convinced that they enjoyed certain higher capacities that entitled them to benevolent treatment. And Henry More, the Cambridge Platonist, while arguing that animals were less valuable than men, also believed them to be possessed of immortal souls.[46]

Clearly Edwards was not inclined to think of animals as mere Cartesian machines. He allowed to them feelings and sensations just as he had to spiders, which could "enjoy" and find "recreation" in their flights. However, cattle, he was convinced, moved not by rational considerations, but by the force of human sounds and the whip. Their behavior was developed by habit enforced by human compulsion. Animals that performed tricks were moved to act by "the habitual association of ideas" derived from "pleasant perceptions of taste"—a comment at variance with his customary reservation of the term *perception* to apply only to human beings. Animal minds ("if I may call them minds") were purely passive, issuing in no truly voluntary actions. Men, on the other hand, possessed passive and active minds and wills, whereby they were fit subjects for "spiritual exercises and enjoyments." Men accordingly were made for religion, whereas animals were not. Yet, in his "Miscellanies" he was to note that, important as religion was to men, still it was contrary to their nature, sin having brought them "nearer to the beast, incapable of religion at all."[47] Only in one respect could animals claim superiority over men. The association of their ideas was much quicker and stronger, "at least in many of them," than that found in humans. But, he concluded, this capacity did not presume any exalted faculty in beasts by which "similar ideas could excite one another."[48]

Lacking as they did a rational faculty, animals could not be expected to know anything of a moral nature. To be sure, when writing of moral taste and beauty, Edwards conceded that God had implanted in them a taste for external beauty akin to moral beauty. In evidence for this judgment he mentioned that "birds have a taste of musick and some serpents will be charmed by mankind." Yet in no way could this instinct be confused with a true virtue, any more than a similar taste for external beauty or a general moral sense in unconverted men be taken for true virtue. Moral sense in some degree may be found in beasts, as in cases of anger and gratitude, but when "our new philosophies" speak of these principles as examples of a moral taste, they fail to see that such a natural moral taste ("if it be proper to call it by this name") in no way approaches that kind of virtue expounded in *The Nature of True Virtue*.[49] Even this similarity between human and animal senses of beauty and morality was played down when Edwards aimed to drive home the differences between men and the brute creation. In defense of the unique character and importance of religious affections, he hotly criticized those who contemptuously regarded these affections as part of "animal nature" or "the brute creation." On the contrary, against the indignity of placing the religious affections on common footing with the lower creation, he proclaimed, they pertained "to the noblest part of the soul."[50]

The foregoing reflections show that Edwards not only was adamantly opposed to any confusion of the lower creation with mankind, but also, in enforcing that conviction, he subordinated the animal kingdom because of its lack of reason and will. In part this subordination was due to Edwards's acceptance of the idea that nature was a hierarchical system, a notion prevalent in the eighteenth century and traceable at least as far back as the Medieval period. This hierarchy was one to be read, as it were, from the top down, not from the bottom upward, as later evolutionist thought would suggest. As Edwards saw nature, God had made man "the head and end of this lower creation," with innumerable creatures having in varying degrees some image of what was in man. Thus animals had more "of a resemblance of what is in man than plants" and "plants much more than things inanimate." Measured by the norm of human capacities, animals occupied a position superior to plants, as did plants above the inanimate creation. In this way what Edwards saw in nature was often not nature in a pristine state, but a nature already structured in his mind by a theory handed down by the culture of his day.[51] Yet the animal creation occupied no mean place in the hierarchy, since it stood closer to man than did either plant life or the inanimate world. In fact, in "Miscellany" 1296 Edwards wrote, "We can conceive nothing more beautiful of an external kind than the beauties of nature here, especially the beauty of the more animated parts of this world"—an opinion that presumably included both animal and plant life.[52] Nevertheless, praise, especially for what he called the brute creation, never rose to the heights of almost ecstatic joy that he lavished upon plants or the features of the inanimate world. In the "Personal Narrative" and his "Diary" it was flowers, clouds, sky, sun, moon, storms, and trees that evoked his deepest religious feelings, not the animal world. The latter he seemed to keep at an intellectual distance.

Like all human beings, Edwards felt nature most closely as a part of himself in his physical body. From his days in the Valley to his final day at Princeton, his body was sublimated to the interests of the mind and his religious faith. His youthful "Diary" plots a course of battles with physical ill health that drastically affected these concerns. As a young man he disciplined and mortified his body so severely that in mature years he was to pay a high price in discomfort and illness. The intensity with which he pursued the life of the mind and his religious interests permanently debilitated him physically. In his youthful zeal for the higher life, he claimed at one point to have surrendered all to the deity. "Neither," he wrote, "have I any right to this body, or any of its members," and he proceeded to enumerate many of his organs and senses that were no longer rightfully his own. "I have given myself clean away, and have not retained any thing as my own."[53] Such exaltation wrested from him those vital energies upon which health depended. He confided to his "Diary" that "too constraint a mortification, and too vigorous application to religion may be prejudicial to health," but he added, "It is no matter how tired and weary I am, if my health is not impaired."[54] Although after a season of mortification he always found "the greatest comforts," he had also to admit that at such times he fell into melancholy and weakness, "decayed in spirituality and lacking energy." "I think," he once wrote, "that I stretched myself farther than I can bear, and so broke."[55] His abstemiousness in eating conspired further to undercut his frail vigor. "I have not been watchful enough over my appetite, in eating and drinking, in rising too late in the morning."[56] He castigated himself for poor eating habits. "This week I have been too careless about eating."[57] He chastised himself for eating intemperately, but admitted that he would eat again shortly thereafter, lest he become faint. Obviously, he was pushing himself too far. This preoccupation with the control of eating he justified by speaking of its effect upon his mental operations, and its value in permitting him to use more time for their exercise. "By sparingness in diet, and eating as much as may be, what is light and easy of digestion, I shall be able to think more clearly and shall gain time."[58] He was clearly of the opinion that the condition and treatment of his physical body deeply affected his moods and spirit. By the time he appeared in Northampton, the excessively strict regimen he had imposed upon himself had taken a toll. His constitution, if we are to believe Dwight, was "so tender and feeble as to be preserved even in tolerable health, only with unceasing care."[59] But we know that he chopped wood for exercise and for the fireplace, and he spoke of riding into the woods for his health.[60] He possessed sufficient vigor to beget a sizable family, and his energy was sufficient to sustain him in his frequent preaching tours away from Northampton.

However, in Stockbridge ill health continued to dog him. At one time, when it was proposed that he shelter several soldiers in his house, he answered by offering to accept only four of them because of his poor health.[61] In a letter to the Reverend Erskine in Scotland he unfolded a litany of sicknesses. He told of fits of ague that seized him, wasting his flesh and strength "until he became like a skeleton." He feared he was falling "into a dropsy."[62] And an important reason he gave for his reluctance to accept the presidency of the College of New Jersey was the precarious state of his mental and physical health. "I have a constitution," he confessed, "in many respects peculiarly unhappy, attended with flaccid solids, vapid, sizy and scarce fluids, and a low tide of spirits." Whatever may have been the original meaning of these quaint words, their total impact described a man in less than vigorous health. To this condition he attributed what he called childish weakness, contemptibleness of speech, presence, and demeanor, disagreeable dullness, and stiffness of manner. It was certainly not an impressive list of qualifications for undertaking the responsibilities of a college.[63] However, by his honesty the Trustees were well forewarned of what might lie ahead if he accepted the office. After an inner struggle, he left Stockbridge for Princeton, where, as mentioned earlier, shortly after entering upon his duties he died of a smallpox inoculation.

In recounting the story of the youthful discipline of his body and his bouts with ill health Edwards nowhere asserted that the physical matter making up his body existed only as an idea. But this fact was always counterpoised by his tendency to exalt the spiritual side of his existence. Unlike many Puritans who followed a heroic ethic that subordinated to the spiritual life the satisfactions of the senses and flesh that come from the hand of God, he had adopted a virtually ascetic mode of living that denied value to his physical nature. His body was more like a burden to be borne than a gift of a beneficent creator to be gratefully enjoyed. So we find him contrasting heaven with earth as a place where no bodies exist. "On earth," he said, men "carry about with them a heavy moulded body, a clod of earth, a mass of flesh and blood that is not fitted to be the organ for a soul inflamed with high exercises of divine love."[64] It is as though no earthly human could experience the true love of God because of his or her physical nature. But his comment also underlines the fact that at one time he did believe in the reality of physical matter. In the revivals some people under the impact of high emotions on their bodies had mistakenly believed them to be signs of divine grace. Opponents of the revivals seized upon this observation as an indication that highly emotional religion was a danger to physical health. Edwards, of course, was forced to answer the charge. He replied that it was a "most specious thing" to claim that "the body is impaired and health wronged" by true religion. "It's hard to think that God, in the merciful influences of his Spirit on men, would wound their bodies and impair their health." If one judged the revivals by the rules of Scripture, there would be no need to get involved with questions of health at all, for "the design of the Scripture is to teach us divinity, and not physic and anatomy." Nevertheless, he did admit that sometimes spiritual blessings overpowered "the nature of man in its present weak state." The feeble body was "not fitted for the views and pleasures and employments of heaven."[65] Undoubtedly when he penned these words he had in mind his own earlier excesses as well as those of people wrought upon in the awakenings.

The relation of the body to the mind, which was one of the important metaphysical and scientific problems of the age, was one that was to bother him throughout his philosophical and religious speculations. In his later writings he pondered this relation, concluding at one point that the union of the two was such that "no lively and vigorous exercise of the will or inclination of the soul" was without effect on the body. By the same laws of union, "the constitution of the body . . . may promote the exercise of the affections," although it did not initiate them. It was not the body but the mind only that was the proper seat of the affections.[66] In the same vein, in "The Mind" he ventured the opinion that "the mind is so united with the body that an alteration is caused in the body, it is probable, by every action of the mind."[67] Yet, in his scientific papers he reminded himself, when he came to speak of the body of man, to demonstrate "the soul's being distinct from matter."[68] As long as Edwards admitted that there actually existed a physical body affected by mental acts, his reference to union of the two was a subterfuge. It did not explain how the body and mind interacted, since in his view they were two very different kinds of being. But for the moment what is important is his willingness to accept as real the human body itself as a part of nature. He could grant priority to the mind or spirit, but he could not make sense of the relation between it and body if the soul was totally distinct from matter. And his whole personal experience of his body's effect upon his mental states was evidence that they were not completely distinct from each other. Those experiences of his own physical nature were as much nature at first hand as were his meditations on the nature about him in the Valley. Nature had not yet been assimilated to idea or symbolism. That was yet to come.

First Law

2

Nature at Second Hand

IN a certain sense nature is always at second hand. We observe it,
enjoy it, fear it, interfere with it, and stand at a distance to interpret
it. However, when I speak of Edwards with nature at first hand I refer
to his naive acceptance of the reality of such natural phenomena as
mountains, valleys, rivers, trees, flowers, and the like. The fact that he
interpreted the impressions of these realities in theological terms in
no way disputes the concrete actualities of nature. What it does show
is how theological culture came into play to give form to the immediacies of firsthand relations to nature. To that degree it can be said
that with the intervention of culture, nature was seen at second hand.
But Edwards had a more unreflective relation to nature by means of
his physical body. Of its pains, appetites, and needs he had no doubt,
although with youthful religious fervor he could say that nothing of it
was his. All was God's. But it was his body that located him in time
and space and made him a part of the corporeal world, to the understanding of which he was to give so much concentrated attention. His
body was of a piece with nature, and his experience of it was certainly
at first hand. His attribution of religious significance to external
nature while generally downgrading the significance of his own body
and finally eliminating matter itself shows that culture in the forms
of theology, science, and metaphysics created a secondhand relation
to nature.

Especially, I speak of Edwards with nature at second hand because
of the impact that scientific and philosophic culture had upon his
views of nature. Science is not a first-order relation to nature. It is the
product of human minds analyzing the behavior of an external world
that stands at a distance from immediate relations to nature. Science,
like metaphysics, is never satisfied with firsthand, surface impressions. Compared to nature at firsthand, it seeks to penetrate the

surface of things to discover the laws or principles by which nature operates. Laws of nature are not nature. They are cultural products. In the same way metaphysics applied to nature stands at a distance from immediately felt impressions of the world and is not nature itself. Both at first hand and second hand the understanding of nature may be counted as productive of profound insights, but in different ways. Hence with Edwards the beauty he found in nature at first hand had deep resonances in his religious nature, as did his search for the laws of nature arrived at by secondhand probing.

This juxtaposition of nature at first and second hand was hinted at in one of Edwards's observations about nature. "He that looks on a plant, or the parts of the bodies of animals, or any other work of nature, at a great distance whence he has but an obscure sight of it, may see something in it wonderful and beyond comprehension, but he that is nearer to it and views them narrowly indeed understands more about them, has a clearer and distinct sight of them." He added that with a microscope one would get "more of a true knowledge concerning them."[1] This passage could easily lead to the supposition that his references to nature in the "Personal Narrative" and parts of his "Diary" were examples of viewing nature from a distance. However, the indelible vigor with which nature imposed itself on him stimulated his religious affections and was anything but obscure. It was "wonderful and beyond comprehension." The nearness to nature and the closer examination of it would be a way of breaking through the mysteries of nature to find its essential principles by scientific and metaphysical examinations. This "truer" knowledge would depend upon a "clearer and distinct sight" of what made nature work. It would be an analysis rather than an appreciation of the surface beauties that firsthand experience had provided. It would be in fact secondhand in the paradoxical sense that the deeper, more exact knowledge of nature was dependent upon the distance at which he as a scientist and philosopher stood in respect to his firsthand experiences of it. The almost mystical romanticism so often attributed to him by modern authors was to give way to an aesthetic appreciation that owed more to the classic lines of geometrical reasonings than it did to the warm, intimate sense of nature that it had given him at first hand.[2]

This distancing of himself from the immediacies of nature does not signify that he had lost all sense of its beauty, which had so filled his mind with nature at first hand. He speculated as a scientist that if it were not for the limitations of the imagination, the creation of the universe out of nothing might be seen as a "wonderful work performed continually," just as it was when "the morning stars sang

ogether."[3] The harmony of all existence was visible all about him in
nature, moving him to entertain thoughts of God's glory and
wisdom.[4] His short essay "Beauty of the World" was so filled with
houghts of beauty and the principles of harmony and propor-
ionality discerned by his metaphysical and scientific mind that, read
oday, it scarcely seems to be a scientific document. Yet it has been
usually included as one of his papers on natural philosophy. Nor is it
unimportant to note that his scientific musings on natural phenomena usually depended on those features of the world with which
ne had been realistically in firsthand contact. Mountains, rivers,
holes in rock, frozen fog, ripples in water, clouds, thunder and lightning, and myriad other things served as occasions for scientific calculations. No matter how abstractly he considered such things, they
were all part of that great whole of nature, of which he intended to
secure a "clearer and distinct sight."

Yet his natural philosophy, as science was called in his day, showed
a shift in attitude and terminology. His dispassionate approach to
nature was scarcely different from that of a secular scientist. And
even the God he praised in these writings was less often a God of
mercy, grace, and love than one whose beauty was expressed in order,
wisdom, and power.[5]

Early in his career Edwards aimed to write "A Rational Account"
hat would demonstrate "how all arts and sciences, the more they are
perfected," would issue in divinity.[6] The strictly scientific part of this
comprehensive project was to be undertaken with a purely objective
attitude with a language suited to such an endeavor. As he con-
templated beginning this task of publication, he set himself a number
of rules by which to discipline his writing. Among these was the use
of plainly stated definitions, postulates, and axioms from which valid
deductions could be drawn. He planned to "extricate all questions
rom the least confusion or ambiguity of words, so that the ideas shall
be left naked." He intended to place axioms at the beginning of trains
of thought, which would be followed by corollaries. These corollaries
often were to bear the weight of theological thought evoked by the
analysis of nature. In accordance with his aim to lay ideas naked, he
also advised himself to "use as few terms of art as I can conveniently."
n short, he proposed to use a deductive procedure couched in spar-
an language shorn of literary adornment and affectation. In these
erms nature was robbed of much of its vibrant reality and, from his
distanced position, it looked increasingly like an orderly geometrical
configuration.

His scientific method of thinking about nature, except where au-
horities were cited, often followed the hypothetical mode of geo-

metrical reasoning. The common formula employed was the pattern of "if this be so" then "thus and so" must follow or be true. Supposition was followed by deductive reasoning, although induction from data also appeared. An extreme but not altogether exceptional example of Edwards's way of thinking is found in his highly speculative account of the manner in which rays of light from stars impinge upon the eye. The demonstration is too long and complicated to be exhibited in its entirety, but the following extract is sufficient. "Suppose," he began, "10,000 [rays from one of the least of the fixed stars] to be within the eye within a third of time." Since fixed stars take up above a sixth minute of the heavens and "a sixth minute being only a 7,797,080,000,000th part of the visible hemisphere," the hemisphere of the eye receiving the rays will also be [a] 7,797,080,000,000th part of the eye. He continued by speculating on the speed of light and its possible obstruction through space, using even more enormous numbers. To check his demonstration, he provided a diagram to show in detail the degrees by which the eye would be affected. He crowned this expedition into the field of astronomy with two corollaries on the skill and art of God in forming the small bodies of light and the eye he had described.[7] Thus, with a theory supported by numbers, perhaps drawn from Derham's report on Huygens, he was laying out the naked ideas of God's laws. Natural philosophy was after all "only to find out the proportion of God's acting."[8]

This dispassionate way of viewing nature was not altogether different from that he used in describing religious experiences. During the revivals he had also managed to stand at a distance from the emotional stirrings he had helped to bring about. His almost clinical observations of the paroxysms and attitudes of new converts were applied to Abigail Hutchison and Phebe Bartlett. Even in his description of his wife's religious experience, he refers to her only in the third person, thus keeping his eye upon the phenomena themselves as proof of the value of the revivals' true religion.[9] He refers to his wife as a person, nameless and sexless. And the same dispassionate, calm poise and discriminating judgment is found in his careful analysis of the affections.[10] On the authority of Samuel Hopkins we are told that the same reserved demeanor obtained even when he was delivering his most dramatic sermons. H. G. Townsend came away from his study of the "Miscellanies" with the opinion that they contained no reference to everyday events or the anguish and joy of daily experiences.[11] If one were to read only Edwards's scientific jottings without any awareness of those expressions concerning a sense of the heart, one would conclude that he had never felt a deep kinship with nature. True, he accompanied his scientific observations and theories with

exclamations of wonder at God's handiwork, but it was more a wonder incited by the marvelous order, symmetry, proportionality, and
harmony of nature, than one that sprang from a heart touched by
gracious affections that went to the depth of the soul.

In part, his attitude toward nature was affected by his knowledge of
British and European scientific authorities. The nature with which a
Newton, Boyle, or Gassendi dealt was an inanimate world, for which
a dispassionate approach was appropriate. Nor was Edwards, as a
Puritan, without intellectual antecedents in the Puritan stream of
thought from an earlier period, which busied itself scientifically with
the examination of nature. Although scholarly opinion has been di-
vided over the role British Puritans played in the development of
science, there is some basis for affirming their part in that enterprise.
Some Puritans had had a hand in the foundation of Gresham College
in 1598, where several of their professors held Puritan convictions.
And the Royal Society, which in one way or another had rootage in
Gresham College, was founded in 1660 to carry on scientific work.
Although not a scientist himself, John Pym as Puritan leader of the
Long Parliament has been considered by some to have been at least
the foster father of that society.[12]

One of the strands that held the Puritans together on the subject of
nature was the conviction, also held by most of the so-called virtuosi
of the Royal Society, that the ways of nature could not contradict
belief in God. However, with the development of science among these
"virtuosi" it became increasingly difficult to conceive a world made
up of corpuscles and atoms moving only by physical attraction consistent with God's sovereign direction.[13] In fact, so formidable did the
problem become that the Royal Society was charged with undermin-
ing Christian revelation and the Bible. The Puritan Richard Baxter
cried out that its members "deny the noblest parts of nature and then
sweep together the dust of agitated atoms and tell us that they have
resolved all the phenomena of nature."[14] Baxter's complaint was not
only over the hubris he detected in the Society's investigations but
also its concentration upon the material and inanimate aspects of
nature, to the disparagement of the higher aspects of the natural
world. Whether or not Edwards had it in mind, it was true that the
science of his day was more interested in the problems of light,
astronomy, physics, and gases pertaining to inanimate nature than in
the biological sciences. However, to balance the record, Charles
Raven, writing in the twentieth century, pointed out that the scientific movement of the seventeenth century "owed more to medicine,
to the study of plants and animals, the development of new foodstuffs
and flowers, and the exploration of new lands and seas, than to

Copernicus and his successors."[15] Yet interest in inanimate nature overshadowed progress in the biological sciences, and Edwards through his readings went mainly with that tide of scientific opinion. The relative paucity of extended or detailed reference to living creatures compared with many references to inanimate creation seems to support that view. Wallace E. Anderson was correct in pointing out that Edwards was unique among colonial scientists of the eighteenth century in that while their contributions were largely in agriculture and medicine, his were primarily in physics.[16] It was there that he found the strongest evidence of God's wisdom and power, although he was to move away from any supposition that the nature described in that field was merely matter.

The treatment of physical nature tended to an emphasis upon structure. The future of science was to depend largely upon the translation of this structure into mathematical formulae, now called the language of nature. Because of his lack of mathematical training, Edwards was not prepared to venture in that direction. But he saw, or believed he saw, that there was a structure of an inclusive kind that appeared when he moved from the structures found within natural phenomena to one structure that embraced all that might be said to exist. Individual items existed in a context where the forms of existence stood in relations of subordination and superordination. Within that context animate as well as inanimate nature had its proper place. Edwards, of course, did not come to this opinion by himself, for the notion of a great chain of being was a familiar one in the thought world of his time. He adopted it as a way of showing how God's wisdom shaped the world. He spoke of the initial chaos of atoms taking on "various and excellent" forms by the laws of matter established by God. This level of beings he counted inferior to "the more excellent work of plants and animals" in whose creation God had exercised a "more immediate hand."[17] Above these animate creations stood mankind and angels, whose unique existence and character occasionally rose above the laws of nature when God acted without intermediate means. He explained that miracles were possible because God was not limited by the laws of nature. If God acted once, he asked, "What is there in nature to disincline [us] to suppose He mayn't continue to act towards the world He made?" And if God continues to act, as He surely does, "then there must be some of His creatures He continues to act upon immediately."[18] In the creation of intelligent beings this immediate and arbitrary divine action was most pronounced. Angels, a case in point, were created immediately and made perfect in their kind all at once, unlike the sun, moon, and stars, minerals, plants, and animals, which were formed out of preexistent principles by a "secondary creation" that presupposed the general laws of nature.[19] Mankind, although lower than angels, had also been dealt with by God apart from the laws of nature by extraordinary and arbitrary actions. It is to the point here to note that Edwards customarily referred to the laws of nature as arbitrary actions of the deity. Nevertheless, he stressed that in the whole graded series of created beings, those who occupied the highest positions came nearer to God. "The nearer we come to God, the less and less we should find that things are governed by general laws, and that the arbitrariness of the supreme cause and governor should be more and more seen."[20] This arrangement was not to be viewed in an evolutionary manner, with the higher forms developing into still higher ones. The direction of creation was from the top down from God, with each set of beings in its own place. After all, as he put it later, "the whole universe, including all creatures, animate and inanimate, in all its actings" proceeded from God with a regard to God as the supreme and last end of all.[21]

Armed with this belief in the structured, hierarchical order of nature, Edwards ordinarily could look upon it as untouched by the consequences of the Fall. All was in order as God had planned and created. However, there were some interpreters of nature who took no such optimistic view. In the seventeenth century Thomas Burnet held that when viewed impartially the world was "a broken and confus'd heap of bodies, plac'd in no order to one another, nor with any correspondency or regularity of parts." The moon "rude and rugged" along with the earth, he opined, was "the image or picture of a great Ruine" and had "the true aspect of a World lying in its rubbish." This world with its rank disorder and disproportion was the result of the degeneracy of mankind.[22] This was obviously not the view Edwards held. From his scientific investigations and reading and yearning for orderliness, he saw the world as essentially an evidence of God's wisdom. It was no chaos or ruin. Neither was it to be an Eden restored by Christ, a world in need of redemption.[23] Yet, as we shall see, it was a world eventually to be swept away in spite of its orderly beauty—but not because of its innate sinfulness. Only perceiving human beings sinned. Nature as such was "dumb" and inert.

The hierarchical system of nature appealed to Edwards's logical mind, yet he was not satisfied until he had penetrated to the "naked ideas" behind and within nature's operations. Whatever principles he would discover were, of course, traceable to God. They would be "the stated methods of God's acting with respect to bodies and the stated conditions of the alteration of the manner of his acting."[24] But what were these principles? Were they detectable only by a mind vividly aware of God? Were they apparent to any rational person, whether or not such a one possessed true religious affections or a sense of the heart? It was a commonplace of theological apologetics in the eighteenth century to argue for God's existence from the evidence of design in nature, although Hume, in his *Dialogues Concerning Natural Religion*, produced damaging criticisms of this strategy. However, it was widely presumed that anyone with common sense and the ability to follow an argument could be convinced that the order found in nature clearly established the existence, wisdom, and power of the deity. The whole purpose of the argument was not simply to shore up the faith of those who did believe, but to convince, without resort to revelation, those who did not believe or were doubtful. This was the direction Edwards took when he set about to establish the unity of God on the basis of the unity of his creation.

The world, he argued, was created and governed to serve one design in all its parts, and in all ages. It was one in which all its members were mutually dependent upon and subservient to each other, and thus by forwarding each other's ends exhibited the one design of the whole. Furthermore, the same laws of nature obtain throughout the universe, showing that there is but one governor. "[Not] only the identity of law in inanimate beings, but in the same sort of animals, especially in the nature of man, in all men, in all ages of the world, shows that all men in all ages are in the hands of the same being."[25] Obviously, anyone could see that the design of the universe in all its parts was the creation of one supreme intelligence. But could one go further to identify the principles at work within this great design? The answer, of course, was in the affirmative, but first some ground had to be cleared, and this was achieved by Edwards's adoption of a form of philosophical idealism.

His interest in the writings of the British scientists and philosophers not only stimulated that interest, but also directed him toward a radical reconsideration of the materialism that in some instances was put forth as the truth about nature. Hobbes, although Edwards probably never read him, was one of those thinkers he mentioned in this connection as having attempted to prove even that God was matter, and that all substance was material.[26] Taken with its mechanistic forms, such a view was, at least in the popular mind, an invitation to irreligion and immorality. To be sure, Edwards accepted to a certain degree the deterministic view of matter common to a mechanistic view of the operation of atoms, but he also limited his enthusiasm for that reading of matter by asserting "There is no such thing as mechanism, if that word is taken to be that whereby bodies act each upon the other, purely and properly by themselves."[27] His idealism would not permit him to be satisfied with a world in which bits of matter were knocked about by an orderly but nevertheless unintelligent physical force.

Accordingly, he took on the tasks of showing that substance, the underlying ground of materialism, was something quite different from what some philosophers and scientists supposed. The pervasive interest in substance was inherited from ancient Greek and Medieval philosophy, in which it was assumed that whatever could be said to exist must depend for its existence and attributes upon some perdurable, underlying substratum. Strict materialists insisted that this substratum was constituted of hard, impenetrable "stuff," while others, like Descartes, bifurcated nature, to use Whitehead's phrase, into two kinds of substance, were baffled by their failure to achieve any scientific knowledge of the structure of this unknown entity.[28] Locke referred to it as "a something we know not what," which was the basis for the modes and relations of thought ascribed to it. But in his attempt to solve the problem of personal identity, he claimed that "nothing but consciousness can unite remote existences into the same person," and "the identity of substance will not do it."[29] Bishop Berkeley caught up Locke's admission that substance was never directly experienced and proceeded to show that on Locke's own empirical principles the notion of any kind of substance was an illegitimate conclusion. He allowed that it was possible to regard bodies as collocations of ideas, but they were not independent of the qualities the mind perceives. Therefore, on his own empirical grounds, there was no need to posit some unexperienceable and indefinable physical substance upon which phenomena depended. Mind alone constituted the world we actually experience. When Hume took up the problem, his skepticism eliminated even the role of the perceiver as one identical being that could stand as mental substance, giving a basis for the unity of the mind. Thus, strictly speaking, since there was no simple impression of the self or the mind, there was no point in accepting either physical or mental substance as the basis for thought.

Edwards was the closest to Berkeley in his treatment of material substance when he accepted the principle that to exist is either to be perceived or to perceive. Existence and perception cannot, nor ought they, be distinguished from each other.[30] However, as Wallace E. Anderson pointed out, Berkeley had argued that matter does not exist—a view Edwards also held—whereas Edwards's attack upon materialism began by arguing that matter was not itself a substance.[31] The substance that philosophers used to think subsisted by itself and stood underneath kept up solidity and all other properties and yet was unknown, was either nothing or the action of God. And, Edwards bitingly commented, if philosophers knew "what they meant themselves," they would see this to be the case.[32] People agree that there has to be some latent substance upholding the properties of bodies, and Edwards admits "there undoubtedly is," but it is not a "something," as Locke called it. "That 'something' is he by whom all things consist."[33] So bodies are kept in space by God, not by some unidentifiable substance or force. Strictly speaking in respect to bodies "there is no proper substance but God himself."[34]

Yet there is some ambiguity in his use of the term *substance*. In a secondary sense he regarded substance as the product of God's action, the effect of "the immediate agency, will and power of God."[35] But in the primary sense of substance, it stood for God in His creative, moment-to-moment activity.[36] He is the ever-active Creator of His world in all its parts, not some inert supporter of bodies.[37] Edwards's predecessors had "thought of substance as the owner of properties," but he "thought of substance as the doer of deeds."[38]

In what then does the apparent physical existence of the universe consist? The answer lay in the consciousness, perception, and knowledge of God. "How doth it grate upon the mind," Edwards exclaimed, "to think that something should be from all eternity, and nothing all the while be conscious of it." The supreme example of this observation was for Edwards the existence of the world in God's knowledge. If one were to suppose that God's consciousness were "intermitted" for a time, the universe would cease to be "because God knew nothing of it." All the figures, magnitudes, motions, and proportions pertaining to the world existed only in God's knowledge of them. "No matter is, in the proper sense, matter."[39] "The world only exists mentally, so that the very being of the world implies its being perceived or discerned."[40]

Here was a metaphysical scheme essentially emergent from epistemological considerations that expressed perfectly both Edwards's spiritual orientation and scientific concern. Substance was God, a spirit and mind, and matter or body was "a particular mode of perception." Things in nature, the more they approached God or the realm of pure idea, "the more properly are they beings, and more substantial. . . ." The correspondence between the terms *more substantial* and *substance* was important, especially since the former hinted at the gradations of being Edwards was to describe elsewhere in his ethics. By the same reasoning, he pointed out, "spirits are much more properly beings, and more substantial, than bodies."[41] He put it even more plainly when he claimed that those beings having knowledge and consciousness are the only proper, real, and substantial beings by whom the being of other things is made effectual. People are grossly mistaken who think material things are the most substantial sorts of things and believe spirits are more like shadows. With a disregard for his identification of substance only with God, he roundly affirmed, "spirits only are properly substance."[42]

In such words Edwards announced the great inversion of what common sense took to be physical nature and matter. Corporeal things exist only mentally and "for most other things, they are only abstract ideas." What men perceived and of which they had ideas were the ideas of God in systematic form. One could be convinced of the truth of what was considered to be "external things" by the consistency of "our ideas" with the ideas of these things presented to us or by "that train and series of ideas, that are raised in our minds according to God's stated order and law."[43] The truth of one's perceptions and ideas lies in their irresistibility, mutual consistency, and orderliness. Fantasies, dreams, and illusions do not have these qualifications, and are thus put out of court. Furthermore, just as Berkeley thought, our ideas of the external world are not the "creatures" of the will. The external world is simply there to be seen without the intervention of any human decision. Since we do not will to see or produce the features of the external world, it must follow that some other spirit or mind produces and sustains them in the absence of human minds, spirit or mind alone being capable of active causation. And this spirit, according to Berkeley, as for Edwards, was God.[44]

As Edwards saw it, truth was the perception of the relations between ideas, whereas falsehood was based on inconsistency among ideas, not in the "disagreement with things" outside the mind. "All truth is in the mind, and only there." Error is explicable only on the grounds of the inadequacy and imperfection of ideas, not as a failure of correspondence with external nature.[45] Truth lay in the logical consistency existing between ideas, whether in human minds or the divine mind. In respect to abstract ideas, truth depended upon "their consistency with themselves," but as to things supposedly outside the mind, truth depended on "the determination, and fixed mode, of God's exciting ideas in us." Truth about nature, then, was the agreement of human ideas with the series of ideas in God's mind. And this was existence, and "that is all we can say." If this system of ideas be followed through, one should conclude that God and real existence were the same.[46]

This identification of real existence and God leads to some curious consequences for Edwards's world view. If ideas alone are real, not matter, and nature is understood as a system of mutually implicative ideas, then nature is not only possessed of real existence, but is God. But that conclusion jars with Edwards's conviction that nature was an inferior realm of shadows and images that reflected the superior supernatural world in which it did not participate. Nature could not then be identified with God or considered to have real existence. As Alfred North Whitehead noted of philosophies that separate a static God from the processing world, "Such philosophies must include the notion of 'illusion' as a fundamental principle—the notion of *mere* appearance."[47] Yet Edwards could not have accepted that conclusion. People do perceive a nature "supposedly outside the mind" which, if still believed to be idea, had the status of objective actuality. People saw flowers, trees, clouds, mountains, and so on, and sensed their own bodies in all their variety and particularity. There might be images and shadows of divine things, but they were not God, that is, they did not have real existence. Yet, as ideas they should be counted as having real existence, not as illusory. Edwards's dilemma was that he could not accept nature as illusory, but neither could he admit that nature enjoyed some other kind of reality than that represented by the identification of God and real existence.

Furthermore, to make God and real existence identical was to threaten the doctrine of creation, which supposed that some kind of being not necessarily identical, but different from God really existed by His creative acts. To think otherwise was to make God all that really existed and to vacate *existence* of all meaning as it pertained to the external world. God alone could be said to really exist, and this state of affairs would be theopantism. Edwards clearly could not settle for that conclusion. His solution to the metaphysical problem was to embrace another form of pantheism known as panentheism. In this theory God was believed to be in all things, but not exhaustively identical with them. Thereby individual items in the corporeal world could be said truly to exist, and yet not be in all respects identical with God. The hierarchical principle, which drew on Neoplatonic imagery, made it possible to conceive the world as composed of various degrees of existence ranging from pure spirit, God, to the limit of nothingness. Between these two extremes entities existed or had being, the amount of which determined their placement in the scale.[48] The closer any entity came to being pure idea or spirit, as we have seen, the closer it came to real substance or God.[49] But since matter did not exist of itself, according to Edwards, there was no place for it on a scale that took only ideas as real. Nature to exist at all must then be a rational set of ideas whose ultimate existence or reality depended on its consistency with the ideas, principles, and laws in God's mind. It could not properly be called divine, yet it had real existence by virtue of its participation in the realm of ideas as projected by God. Nature was not in its own essential character spiritual. That attribute pertained only to perceiving human beings and to God. However, as an inferior dimension of God's creation it was perceptible and knowable, and therefore real in some secondary sense. Nature, as Edwards lamely put it, was "supposedly outside the mind," but he insisted it was actually in the mind of men and God. This was the nature Edwards proposed to exhibit as consisting "in things being precisely according to strict rules of justice and harmony."[50] But difficulties, as already suggested, awaited his attempt to read nature in uncompromisingly idealistic terms.

Edwards never provided a systematic catalogue of the principles that insured the justice and harmony of nature, in part because they were so closely entangled with each other that, for instance, to mention harmony was to bring along all the other principles in its train. Two of Edwards's shorter works may be used to identify some of these principles. In the "Beauty of the World" he delineated several elements by which he understood that the beauty "peculiar to natural things" surpassed the art of man. His overriding aim was to show how the beauties of nature resembled spiritual beauties, but to accomplish this end he had first to show that beauty existed in nature. So in nature he saw a profusion of "consents" among various things, agreements of parts with wholes and agreements of wholes with wholes. In nature's colors he found "complicated proportion." In its sounds the proportion of vibrations accounted for audibility. In light there was "harmony and proportion," just as there was "harmonious motion" in the "proportionate mixture" of the color white. This insight Edwards apparently borrowed from Newton.[51] In the "Wisdom in the Contrivance of the World" he dwelt on the consummate order with which God had ordered the atmosphere, the human eye, the orb of the earth and the placing of the planets. God's world was one of intelligible order that showed His wisdom and power.[52] In his other scientific and metaphysical writings Edwards rang the changes on these themes and expanded upon them with the addition of other principles. Harmony, for example, was impossible without relationality and its counterpart, attraction, among the parts of nature. "Two beings," he claimed, "can agree one with another in nothing else in relationship. . . ."[53] This fundamental truth he used to explain personal identity and the identity of all mankind with Adam, when he wrote of original sin.[54] In respect to nature, relationality and attraction were evident in the way atoms operated. He surmised that "the least atom" by its existence and motion "causes an alteration, more or less, in every other atom in the universe," thus making the universe "all over different from what it would otherwise have been."[55] Apparently he hoped, at one time, to demonstrate this to be the case, although he never did so.[56] Similarly he intended to show how "the least wrong step in the least atom, happening never so seldom, if it returns at a certain period, would most certainly . . . totally subvert the order of the universe."[57] For this emphasis upon relationality and mutual attraction he may well have found support in the writings of John Henry Bisterfield. According to that author "no being is solitary; all being is symbiotic. . . . All things are essentially related to other things."[58] This would have been a view with which Edwards had the deepest sympathy, for it was foundational to the agreements and consents that he found in nature.[59]

Edwards was an atomist not only because he treated of atoms as a scientist, but also because as a metaphysician he drew from the idea of atomicity an explanation of the relations and distinctions among other kinds of entities. The world was idea and constituted an orderly system, but it was not therefore a monad in which the elements of nature or different kinds of being coalesced into a numerical or ontological unity. At this point another basic principle of nature comes into view, that of polarity. Polarity made possible an intelligible rendering of agreement and consent. In his extended analysis of excellence he contended for relation as the basis for beauty, but for such relation to exist there must be distance or distinction between two or more entities. When the distance is one of equality, there is then relation, and this relation between two bodies is their correspondence to each other, which results in beauty. Otherwise, where there is a lack of similarity of relation, deformity occurs. *Deformity* is a term borrowed from the conception of physical shape, and was one of Edwards's favorite words for moral evil or sin. It begets disagreeableness rather than agreeableness in perceiving beings, it being contrary to or at odds with the nature of being itself, which is harmonious. In fact, according to Edwards, it is "the greatest and only evil."

As with bodies, so with perceiving beings; there must be a relation of similarity and agreement, but this relation cannot be one in which two beings are identical in the literal sense of that term. The relation may be identical; the two beings cannot be. Hence the principle of polarity: "Two beings can agree one with another in nothing else but relation: because otherwise the notion of twoness (duality) is destroyed and they become one."[60] Without this polarity relationality would have made no sense, and without it the principle of a harmonious universe would have been lost and, with it, excellence at all levels of being. Polar relations protected the status of individual entities (atoms), both in nature and in the ethical and spiritual realm (selves) from a sterile, all-encompassing monism.

The principle of polarity was so important to Edwards that he incorporated it in his conception of God as the Trinity. "One alone cannot be excellent," he wrote, inasmuch as, in such a case, "there can be no consent." Therefore, he concluded "if God is excellent"— and for him there was no doubt on that score—"there must be a plurality in God: otherwise there can be no consent in Him."[61] And without consent God could not exercise the consent to himself that is love. "His infinite beauty is his infinite mutual love of himself."[62] Nor is it beyond reasonable supposition that Edwards's reluctance to allow saints to be mystically absorbed into the deity owes something to the same principle of polarity. He argued that although God aimed at an infinitely perfect union between the creature and himself, "the particular time will never come when it can be said, the union is now infinitely perfect."[63] This was a devotional rendering of what he had expressed metaphysically when he wrote, "there is no proportion between finite beings, however great, and universal being."[64] However, in Miscellany 150 he had written "if we should suppose the faculties of a created spirit to be enlarged infinitely, there would be the deity to all intents and purposes."[65] Nevertheless, in the main, duality or polarity still obtained.

The discussion of polarity returns us to the importance of consent and agreement in Edwards's thought. Excellence was "the consent of being to being, or being's consent to entity." The more extensive this consent was, the greater the excellence and beauty.[66] Without polarity consent would be impossible, and without consent there would be no excellence. As applied to the natural world, consent was the organic element that held all together, as did mutual attraction. The world of sensible objects for Edwards was indeed one in which harmonious tunes, or the strokes of penmanship, were like a society of perceiving beings "sweetly agreeing together," giving "the appearance of consent."[67] In the beauty of pen sketches of flowers, the human body, and facial features, and in the harmony of musical notes there are consent and proportion. It is as though the parts "loved one another," making up "an image of love in all the parts of a society united by a sweet consent and charity of heart."[68] Although these examples of consent were drawn from the sensible world, Edwards insisted that they were but "the shadows of excellency." They were like love, but not really love. The consent among them "gave the appearance of perceiving and willing being."[69] It was a world where the consents among earthly things were merely images of a higher world, where true excellency existed. This way of construing the sensible world obviously depended not on the observation of natural objects and their relations, but on the imposition by Edwards of his philosophical idealism.

Consent among sensible objects was nevertheless important to Edwards's case. Nature actually did exhibit what he called agreement or consent. However, the shift in language by the use of the word *love* applied to the constituents of the sensible world indicated that he wished to imply an idea far richer in content than a harmonious and naturalistic agreement among phenomena. It was a shift from thoughts about nature and sensible objects to thoughts about spiritual things. This transition he made clear when he admitted that the word *consent* was borrowed from spiritual things, since in a proper sense consent could occur only between minds or wills.[70] We need not doubt Edwards's sincerity in claiming that the notion of consent was derived from the spiritual realm or that consent embodied love, but we can doubt whether in fact that was the direction his mind took. There was altogether too much metaphysical reasoning on nature that had gone into his analysis of excellence to accept his admission at face value.

It is significant that his description of excellence was couched in impersonal entities expressed by geometric diagrams.[71] He did not, to be sure, turn to contemplation of perceived nature, but instead moved directly to considerations of abstract structure that he found in nature. Excellency, he argued, was made up of "harmony, symmetry or proportion," and proportion was constituted of "equality or likenesses of ratios." Simple equality between things without proportion was the lowest kind of regularity, into which "all other beauties and excellencies may be resolved." When proportion is added, complex beauty results; where proportion or similarity of relations is lacking, the result is a "disagreeableness to perceiving beings because there is disarray or disjunction in respect to being itself." The opposite condition promotes pleasure. Now, throughout nature the principles of correspondence, symmetry, regularity, equality, and proportion obtain. As examples Edwards listed the beauty of flowers, the bodies of men and animals, rivers, plants and trees, showing that their beauty consisted of a "very complicated harmony." In the same manner the motions, tendencies, and figures of "bodies in the natural universe" were due to a proportion wherein their beauty also existed. He allowed that disproportions did exist, but they only added to general beauty when set in the context of a more extensive, universal proportion. Of course, following his religious and philosophical bent, he insisted that spiritual harmonies, where proportions were redoubled and affected more beings, were more important than those found in such natural phenomena as light, colors, tastes, smell, and touch. But the reason all these gave pleasure to human beings was that they were consistent with being. What was being at this stage of his analysis? "Being, if we examine narrowly, is nothing else but proportion."[72] In fact, he affirmed, "we find nothing that the mind loves in things but proportion."[73] Proportion runs throughout the world, both natural and spiritual. "The proportion is with the whole series of acts and designs from eternity to eternity."[74]

The principle of proportionality was so important to Edwards that he made it one of the tests of true religious affections. Lest affections run off into chaotic passions and structureless "enthusiasms," he laid it down that false affections were to be identified by their lack of "entireness and symmetry of parts," while truly gracious affections exhibited "beautiful symmetry and proportion."[75] Thus the dynamics of the soul, no less than of nature, were to pay tribute to proportion as the form Edwards held to be essential to the order and harmony of the world as a whole. And finally, this attachment to proportionality was to bear fruit by structuring Edwards's ethics. Even love itself, the highest of ethical values, was to be subject to proportion in delineating how people seem to behave and think.

However, in one major respect the principle of proportionality did not apply. There was a fixed limit between mankind and God. "There is no proportion between finite being, however great, and universal being."[76] But, as in the case of the Trinity, where God loves Himself in proportion to His own greatness of being, proportion was not set aside. And if being was "nothing else but proportion," then the proportion found in the world did have an important part in the spiritual world as well. Spiritual being must then be congruent in some way with worldly being if the latter was to reflect the spiritual truths and graces Edwards insisted it held. Whether one gives priority to the realm of finite and corporeal being or prefers to emphasize the spiritual domain when seeking religious truth, the gap between the two dimensions was not so enormous that nothing could be said about either from the standpoint of the other. The ontological status of each dimension was for Edwards different from that of its opposite number, but there was a connection of formal relations that made intercourse possible between them.

Thus we come upon another of Edwards's favorite principles, that of analogy. The use of analogy in respect to nature was not unique to his thought. For centuries people had imposed symbolism upon nature and found in it examples of virtues and vices, all without any necessary connection with the type of philosophical idealism Edwards favored. One did not have to embrace his strict antimaterialistic outlook to discover spiritual equivalences to nature. A materialist could be beguiled to think of nonmaterial things in the presence of nature or perceive analogies between the external and internal worlds without absolutizing those reflections into some superior self-existent world. Belief in an order of ideal Platonic forms either supervening upon or structuring nature was not a necessary concomitant for appreciating the physical world or finding richer meanings than lay on its surface. Even an atheist could be moved by nature to contemplate peace, beauty, and order, and even to descry some moral truth without commitment to theism or metaphysical idealism. But not so for Edwards.

For him analogy had to be grounded in nature along with an idealism that negated matter. His analogical treatment of the finite world was not based solely on the recognition that the human mind was limited and had therefore to take recourse to analogy to understand what nature taught. Granted the mind's finitude, it did not follow that the use of analogy was a mere epistemological device to get around a difficult problem. In this respect Edwards moved in a different direction from Bishop Butler, who defended analogy as a reliable way of ascertaining the truth of the Christian religion. In his *Analogy of Religion* Butler claimed that when an event is like some other event, the mind determines it to be probably true or morally certain that the second event, otherwise unknown, is true or factual by virtue of the strong resemblance it has to the first surely known event. Therefore he concluded that "probable evidence, in its very nature, affords but an imperfect kind of information." For God things and events were certain, not probable, but for mortals probability based on analogy was the best one could reasonably expect. To us, "probability is the very guide of life." Analogy was "evidently natural, just and conclusive."[77]

At one point Edward seems to have accepted a view like that of Butler when he explained that the names of spiritual things were for the most part derived from sensible or corporeal ones, because there was no other way of making people understand meanings except by analogy.[78] This statement is in accord with my thesis because it is a straightforward admission that as a practical matter nature is necessary to understanding spiritual language. Thus analogy seems to be used here as it was by Butler as a way of surmounting a knotty epistemological problem. In the main, however, Edwards was not content to stake his case for analogy upon either probability as a guide to the spiritual dimensions of nature or as a practical concession to limited human knowledge. He desired a certainty that was more than a conclusion made by finite minds otherwise unable to discern spiritual realities. Analogy for him was a reality permeating all parts of God's creation. God had created the world in the mode of analogy and consequently the certainty Edwards sought was to be found everywhere. Analogy was the created necessary link "in the bodies of all animals, and in all plants and in the different parts of the inanimate creation,"[79] and among the notes for "The Mind" he proposed to examine "the manifest analogy between the Nature of the Human Soul and the Nature of other things."[80] In his *Original Sin*, after affirming God's wisdom in the "beautiful *analogy* and *harmony* of his constitution and laws," he claimed that Adam and his posterity were linked together by God's arbitrary constitution. "There is an apparent manifold analogy" in the case of this constitution "to other constitutions and laws, established and maintained through the whole system of vital nature in this lower world. . . ." And since the first of kind in nature was the source of all subsequent properties and qualities, there could be no perfection in them that was not in their source. Hence, by analogy Adam's posterity did not enjoy the original righteousness of Adam, since he had lost it. All of which, Edwards concluded, was "analogous to other laws and establishments" relating to the nature of mankind.[81]

The dialectics of analogy were here seriously strained, but it is impossible to overlook the confidence Edwards deposited in the principle of analogy as existing both within nature and between nature and spiritual matters. This confidence in analogical reasoning was further shored up by the comments of George Turnbull, an author criticized on other grounds by Edwards in *Original Sin*. Turnbull had observed that "no words can express moral ideas but so far as there is an analogy betwixt the natural and moral world." Analogy makes "the beauty, propriety, and force of words expressive of moral ideas by conveying pictures of them into the mind." Turnbull's metaphysic and epistemology differed widely from that of Edwards, but the latter seized gratefully upon Turnbull's insights. "There is a much more exact correspondence and analogy between the natural and moral world," Turnbull thought "than superficial observers are apt to imagine or take account of."[82] But Edwards, in no superficial manner, had taken account of these analogies and made them the basis of understanding the moral and spiritual realm. God's creation was replete with analogies that were not simply accidental similarities, but ingredients of the holistic structure of all being. God, as a dynamic deity, was all the time creating and maintaining this relation between the physical and spiritual domains. Therefore there was an "actual metaphysical connection between the perceived world and divine activity."[83] Or as George S. Hendry argued, nature did not accidentally happen to resemble spiritual realities, but rather exhibited "an ontological continuity, or congruity between the worlds of nature and spirit." There was a deep underlying affinity between the two,[84] which is to say that that was the way God had created and was creating both the corporeal and the spiritual world in respect to each other.

Nature viewed metaphysically and scientifically was a harmonious entity dependent upon relationality, agreement or consent, proportionality, mutual attraction, and analogy. This array of dominant principles reflected the distance at which Edwards stood from nature, but they were essential ingredients of its beauty. "When we think of the sweet harmony of the parts of the corporeal world," he exclaimed, "it fills us with such astonishment that the soul is ready to break."[85]

In spite of his admiration of God's work in nature, biblical eschatology dictated that this beauty would be destroyed at the end of history. Strictly speaking, nature was not ultimately to be redeemed, if even that term is deemed appropriate for a nature that elsewhere in Edwards' writings seems to have been just as God had created it. Now, in the context of eschatology the view of nature was made totally subservient to the eternal destiny of the saints. The noble grandeur of corporeal nature was not only subservient to the spiritual value, but decidedly inferior to what God planned for the soul. "Senseless matter, in whatever excellent order it is placed," Edwards thought, "would be useless if there were no intelligent beings at all, neither God nor others."[86] His philosophical idealism thus triumphed over any suppositions that nature was independently worthy of continued existence. In fact, this corporeal world was running down toward its inevitable destruction. "Does God," he asked, "make the world restless . . . to make no progress . . . only to come to the same place again, to be just where it was before?" Obviously not, for Edwards did not accept a cyclical view of nature as a whole. Rather, the world was on its way by the depletion of its resources, but there were cycles within nature. The sun goes round and round, the seas are restless, the heart and lungs continue to react, the blood circulates, the body is replenished by food and sleep, as is the earth by rain and snow, but to what end? After all these revolutions, what remains of the whole? All these bodies are expending and wasting themselves, a fact that shows that "the whole universe is corruptible and must come to an end."

The world that appeared so beautiful and harmonious even after the Fall was at last no "paradisiacal" place. After that debacle, as far as man was concerned, "the place of paradise was . . . changed from earth to heaven, and God ordered it so that nothing paradisiacal should be any more here." Only the shadow of paradise remained in the world. And lamentably "those things that look most paradisiacal will have some sting to spoil them." Earthly attachments, even the sense of nature's beauty, will vanish in the world's denouement. But human souls as saints will survive this catastrophe, else God's purpose would be frustrated and brought to naught. The divine glory and honor would not be beheld unless "the inanimate, unperceiving part of the world" were regarded as subservient to the "perceiving and intelligent parts" of the world. With the final destruction of nature, saved intelligent beings will inevitably know and be satisfied with the great design that God had in mind in the whole changing pattern of the universe.[87] "Wherefore religion must be the end of creation, the great end, the very end."[88]

The "Personal Narrative" associated Edwards's early religious experiences with nature. Its brooding solitude enveloped him when he drew apart to meditate and pray. Sun, moon, stars, clouds, blue sky, grass, flowers, trees, water, and thunder storms evoked "sweet" thoughts and contemplations of Christ, God, and salvation. These realities were specific items of his experience, not generalities or abstractions. It was not their overall order that first impressed him, but their concrete impact, summoning up devotional emotions that so pervaded his consciousness that he broke into song in a low voice. It is not easy to set aside the conviction that those same natural phenomena incited in him the desire to give a more rational and scientific account of his environment. In a practical sense they were the first data from which his metaphysics of nature developed.

However, the nature reshaped as it was by Edwards's acquaintance with British and Continental authors was a quite different nature from that which had stirred his evangelical religious sentiments. Under the spell of scientific and metaphysical rationalism the details and particularities of nature came to be subsumed under the stark simplicity of God's laws of order. The harmony of nature continued to arouse his sense of beauty. It was a beautiful world, it was God's world, but it revealed less His favor, grace, and salvation than it did His wondrous creating, ordering, and harmonizing power in the corporeal world. Divine elements in nature were systematized into general patterns subject to laws or principles. The aimless fecundity, the rampant irregularity, and the sheer novelty of nature had no place in this view. Edwards seemed to have forgotten that no two leaves of a plant, no two flowers on a stalk, no two snowflakes, clouds, mountains, rivers, or animals were precisely alike in shape or content. The nonrepeatable sequences of nature and hence its novelty were set aside in favor of scientific orderliness, and something of the mystery of nature was lost. The vitality of nature was surrendered to the exigencies of rational intelligibility. Even when on occasion Edwards dealt with living nature, he seemed baffled until he had reduced it to regularity. The growth of trees from seed fixed his mind on what seemed to be an exception to the natural order. He waxed enthusiastic about what was wonderful about trees "beyond anything that is to be found in the inanimate world." Their diversification into branches, leaves, flowers, fruits, and seeds, going on from age to age, fascinated him. Yet there was a problem. The tree "most certainly don't keep its rule, don't exactly follow its copy in the seed." If trees always grew in the same regular order, matters would be simpler and more comprehensible. However, "the branches of the tree seem not capable of being reduced to any rule at all, but there is an infinite variety; one branch grows out here, another there, without any order." This diversity and irregularity nevertheless he immediately reduced to order. When trees and plants first begin, they are "exactly regular." Then buds stand in a regular and uniform manner, and as the tree or plant grows, the branches come out in positions opposite to each other, "always standing transverse to the former two." This, according to the diagram he sketched, applied to maple trees, while the branches of certain fruit trees appear one at a time on different sides "in such order as to stand round the twig in the form of a screw." Because the first sprouts of the tree are always regular, "so are all the young sprouts of the tree afterward." He triumphantly concluded, "it follows that the body, the main branches, and the little twigs, and every part of every tree in the world, in their first beginning, were regular."[89] Order and regularity at last overcame the apparently riotous diversity of growing things. Multiplicity existed in nature, but when properly observed and speculated upon, heterogeneity fell within the borders of an order to which there were no exceptions. It was a nature consisting "in things precisely according to strict rules of justice and harmony."[90]

Had not Edwards been seduced by his stress on inanimate nature and by the prestige of foreign scientific and philosophical authorities to forget the details of nature that under other conditions had deeply impressed him by their uniqueness? His search for "naked ideas" had stripped nature of its remarkable diversity and effectively anatomized it. Of the eighteenth century Gerald R. Cragg truly commented, "Nature's order seemed so clear that men were tempted to forget its ambiguities."[91] At times the nature of the Valley seems to have become only a distant memory for Edwards.

3

The Ambiguities of Nature

THE ambiguity of nature appears in the fact that when it is observed at first hand no two of its parts or actions are exactly alike, whereas when viewed at second hand its behavior is seen as completely orderly and expressive of regularities that are formulated as laws. These laws for the most part do not take into account the uniqueness of single entities, but depend for their validity on the measured composite behavior of a number of individual entities. Thus nature, depending on the position of the observer, offers two different faces. Edwards's description of trees is a good example of the transformation that can be made from the uniqueness of each tree's growth into the regularity of the natural order of trees in general. However, an additional ambiguity in respect to nature appears when, as with Edwards, nature is itself interpreted in terms of philosophical idealism. As pure ideality it is easier to describe nature's orderliness as the consistency of ideas with each other when physical matter is dispensed with. But the question remained as to the status of nature when viewed at first hand, compared with nature at second hand.

What Edwards had done in adopting idealistic phenomenalism was to set apart a nature made up of corporeal bodies and a nature that was entirely the result of mind, human and divine. It was in some respects a world understood on the Lockean model, in which spatiotemporal qualities were primary and to which the mind attributed such secondary qualities as sound, scent, color, pain, and the like.[1] This bifurcation of nature at the outset was to be the fertile source of the ambiguities in his view of nature. It was a perspective later to be attacked in Whitehead's philosophy of organism, in which human experience was made a part of nature itself. "Our experiences of the apparent world," wrote this twentieth-century philosopher, "are nature itself."[2] But this was not Edwards's answer to the Lockean conception of nature.

His answer was one closer to that of Berkeley, who ruled out Locke's primary qualities as having any independent reality, and deposited nature in the mind. Nature never shows itself as having primary qualities without secondary ones. There is never quantity without quality, and therefore mind is the integral element without which nature would not exist.[3] This idealistic philosophy was essentially an epistemological approach to nature that overcame the separation of mind and body conceived as inert matter, and it continued in one form or another to color all future attempts to work out a metaphysics of nature. The question of knowledge henceforth had to be settled before one could get at nature itself. Nature as interpreted by the mind was real nature, but nature as a firsthand impact on the self, as in the "Personal Narrative" and parts of the "Diary," was not to be enjoyed in its own right. Instead, we were given a descriptive psychology of what in common-sense terms was called nature. The difference between appearance and reality was nullified by identifying the one with the other, or more exactly, eliminating the difference entirely. To know nature was to see it as a network of ideas and perceptions in which each set of ideas suggested others in a regular order.[4]

How far Edwards was directly influenced by Berkeley has been the source of lively debate. Perry Miller forthrightly claimed that there was no evidence that Edwards had ever read Berkeley,[5] a view to which Wallace E. Anderson also subscribed at one time when he stated that Edwards was not a disciple of Berkeley, but developed his views independently of him.[6] Later, however, Anderson offered evidence that Edwards had read Berkeley's *An Essay Toward a New Theory of Vision* and he noted that this book and Berkeley's *Principles of Human Knowledge* were included in Edwards's "Catalogue."[7] George Rupp, however, claimed it to be "baseless" that Berkeley had influenced Edwards.[8] The most extreme view of the connection between Edwards and Berkeley was offered by Émile Bréhier, who said that Berkeley knew Edwards or his works, and that Edwards had spread his ideas in America.[9] In this the French philosopher was certainly wide of the mark. We know that Edwards read Locke, and the probability is that he read some parts of Berkeley, but it is also true that he differed from both in significant ways.[10] He was a slavish follower of neither, although there has been a tendency to exaggerate the influence of Locke upon him.[11]

As we trace out again Edwards's view of nature, we find not only similarities to Berkeley, but also those ambiguities which cast doubt on the success of his effort to construe it in terms of mind. Nature for him was a system of ideas and perceptions. Thus, when confronted with the charge that immaterial substance gave no indication of its independent existence, he flatly answered, "all existence is perception," and material body is "nothing but a particular mode of perception." Spirit, on the other hand, was "nothing but a composition and series of perceptions." This statement was scarcely helpful in suggesting what the difference was between the two kinds of perceptions, but he maintained that the universe was "a coexisting and successive" set of perceptions connected by the "wonderful methods and laws of the deity."[12] This theme of connected perceptions with the ideas that they stimulated was to resound throughout his scientific and philosophical writings.

Edwards repeatedly emphasized that the natural world was "absolutely dependent on idea."[13] Put in a slightly different way, the material world was "absolutely dependent on the conception of the mind for its existence. . . ." Spirits, on the other hand, did not depend on "the conception of other minds."[14] In consequence, bodies "have no proper being of their own."[15] In essence Edwards was giving a negative answer to the question he posed in Miscellany pp. There he asked "in what respect has anything a being when there is nothing conscious of its being?"[16] Without consciousness there would be nothing, and nothing, as he had demonstrated, was "horrid nonsense" and utterly impossible to conceive.[17] Of course there was something, and above all it was mind.

The fundamental principle of his idealism made nature's existence dependent upon perception and consciousness. But here lay an epistemological ambiguity. Was perception or consciousness a causal category? Did perception or being aware of something cause it to exist? From the fact that no one could be aware of something without its being coincidentally in existence it did not follow logically that the existence of the object was due to its being perceived or known. Much depends at this point on how Edwards conceived causation. He had defined cause as "that, after or upon the existence of which, or the existence of it after such a manner, the existence of another thing follows."[18] He had worked out this idea of causation to good effect in the "Freedom of the Will," where in large degree he adopted a position similar to that of Hume. Cause was the connection or conjunction between events in which an antecedent was connected with a consequent event rather than being an efficient cause of it. In that work he was intent on showing that free acts were uncompelled acts, not uncaused or undetermined acts.[19] Therefore, if we are to take over Edward's idea of causation in respect to perception, there would be a simple constant connection between perception and the existence of natural phenomena, rather than an instance of perception as efficient causation compelling natural phenomena to exist. However, it is important to notice that his definition of cause presupposes a temporal sequence of something existing after an antecedent event. Perception, on the other hand, as the cause of existence, is instantaneous. To perceive and to exist constitute one coincidental action. The existence of whatever is said to exist does not depend on a temporal sequence, and in this sense Edwards clearly assumed that perceiving something caused it to exist, in the older meaning of efficient causation. Both Edwards and Berkeley seem to have assumed this point; to be is to be perceived—and built their respective philosophies on this assumption. Furthermore, insofar as Edwards's thought paralleled that of Berkeley, he had nowhere established that all existence was mental. All either of them could say was that what men actually perceived or of which they were conscious were qualities, not objects or things as such. Qualities may well indeed exist relative to percipients, but it does not logically follow that some things or entities could not exist unless a percipient was present. Cryptically stated, it could be affirmed that there was nothing illogical in claiming that unperceived physical objects might exist, even though it was impossible to perceive an instance of this being the case empirically.[20]

Of course he understood the epistemological situation differently, and he was acutely aware of the argument that something real actually existed apart from a percipient. He bent his efforts to show that at least logically such could not be the case. The notion that something existed without there being perception or consciousness was for him the product of a misinformed imagination. "Our imagination makes us fancy we see shapes and colors and magnitudes, though nobody is there to behold it." This would be a contradiction from the very beginning because the shapes, colors, and magnitudes would already be in the mind. Edwards offered several examples in respect to color, solidity, and resistance that to him called for the existence of a percipient and the presence of idea. On resistance he argued that it was as easy to conceive "resistance as a mode of an idea" as it was to conceive of idea as stopping or resisting color. "The idea may be resisted—it may move, and stop, and rebound; but how a mere power which is nothing real can move and stop is inconceivable, and it is impossible to say a word about it without contradiction." He then concluded: "The world is therefore an ideal one."[21] Apart from the fact that his conclusion was faulty, the language used about ideas resisting, moving, stopping, and rebounding seems to make no sense except as presenting analogies to physical entities and powers, such as gravity. The argument certainly was less than convincing to establish that mental operations were necessary for existence.

A better case offered was based on dual suppositions. One, that in a room closed up where no one sees or hears anything, there are still the effects on others of what is in the isolated room, because, to return to Edwards's dominant theme of relationality, "there is not one leaf of a tree, nor spire of grass, but what has effects all over the universe, and will have to the end of eternity." Second and more important, the closed-up room is itself only in God's consciousness. Edwards then asked his readers to imagine the impossibility of one's consciousness, and especially God's, to be interrupted for a period of time. "I say, the universe for that time would cease to be, of itself; and not only . . . because the Almighty would not attend to uphold the world, but because God knew nothing of it." And after this imaginative flight offered in support of his argument, Edwards dared to write, " 'Tis our foolish imagination that will not suffer us to see!"[22] The answer he offered to the puzzle concerning the metaphysical status of qualities, properties, and entities when no human consciousness was present was to repeat in his own way Berkeley's answer. God's consciousness and knowledge upheld the existence of all that was beyond human awareness at any particular time. The move saved his philosophical idealism. He did not want to claim that human consciousness alone created and preserved the world, so he concluded that only a divine, infinite power could bring bodies into being and sustain them. No created being could do this.[23]

What he had done, however, was to transfer to God what he held to be true about the existence of bodies and qualities within the world where human consciousness operated. Thus he made the existence of all of the universe in all its parts, even where human consciousness was unable to penetrate, dependent on God's awareness of it. However, this step was no more convincing than his original position in regard to the existence of things in the world due to human consciousness. However, it does show how important his epistemology was in fashioning his metaphysics.

Two others of his ruling principles might have led him to a different conclusion regarding the importance of consciousness and knowledge. The first of these is the principle of polarity embodied in his insight that two beings could agree with each other only by relation "because otherwise the notion of their twoness (duality) is destroyed and they become one."[24] This principle, if consistently adhered to in respect to bodies and minds and man's relation to God leads inexorably to the conclusion that reality must itself be composed of at least two kinds of existence. Polarity could well apply to the difference between two ideas, but it could as well apply to the distinction between nature and mind. Certainly, if used in respect to nature,

polarity demanded that it not be made one with human consciousness lest "twoness" be destroyed. An equally important metaphysical principle was enunciated in respect to excellence. "One
alone, without reference to any more, cannot be excellent."[25] If excellence has any reference to nature, and it seemed to do so in Edwards's
chants about its beauty, then no monism of an ideal type properly
obtained. There had to be "twoness," not a monism, unless he surrendered one of his basic principles. He salvaged these two principles by
embracing atomism within nature and emphasizing the lack of proportionality between finite existence and God. To this degree polarity
overcame a strict monistic outlook, but in fact he never drew the
conclusion I have drawn from the two principles. Instead, he tena-
ciously clung to the all-absorbing priority of the mind and consciousness.

Nevertheless the two principles operated when he distinguished
the spiritual and mental aspects of reality from nature. His language
betrayed the fact that there was a duality between nature and mind
for which it was difficult to account. He was not so far lost in his
idealistic phenomenalism as to lose all contact with the realities of
common-sense empiricism. If he was to avoid sheer illusionism, he
had to pay attention to what he actually experienced and assumed to
be true of other conscious beings. He had to do business with a realm
of experience whose objectivity of content depended on something
more than ideas entertained in the mind.[26] And this fact showed up
in the language he was forced to use. He could speak of such things as
an "external or material world" in which there were "solidity of
bodies, drops of water, brains, earth, birds and even particles diffused
from celestial bodies etc." He could even assign a location to the mind
when he wrote "thought is not properly in matter, though it be in the
same place," although he also expressed doubt as to whether
"thought can be in a place."[27] And he gave credit to body as the
medium by which spirit communicated to selves. Nor was there any
other medium of acting on other creatures or being acted upon by
them, than the body. Even Satan could produce no effect upon men's
souls except by the body.[28] On the other hand, he reminded himself
when writing about the body to "let the demonstration of the soul's
being distinct from matter be inserted."[29] If language is a clue to
understanding a philosophical position, then it is clear that a duality
existed between nature as immediately experienced and nature re-
worked in idealistic terms.

Edwards lavished words of praise on God's creation of the natural
world. Its beauty, proportion, and harmony stirred him, giving rise to
religious sentiments of the deepest profundity. However, the other

side of the coin was his deprecation of this same world. This material world, he claimed, was senseless and useless except in subordination to and dependence upon the perceiving and knowing part of the creation. "What could this vast universe of matter . . . be good for," he inquired, "if there were no intelligence that could know anything of it?"[30] The inanimate, unperceiving part of the world "is nothing if regarded otherwise than in subserviency to the perceiving or intelligent parts."[31] Animate bodies such as beasts might be regarded as part of the perceiving creation[32] but they, in Edwards's opinion, were downgraded also because they lacked the spiritual capacities that made possible religion, which was the purpose of the whole creation.[33] It is noteworthy in these statements that Edwards used the words *material* and *matter*, although we know he elsewhere denied that matter existed. But for him the properties of matter, translated into idealistic terms, were solidity, extension, resistance, and so on, and were as such as much ideas as were color or pain. They were qualities of the mind.[34] This world, he concluded, is an ideal one and "all material existence is only idea."[35]

Why then do men mistakenly persist in believing nature to be composed of matter when material things are not the most substantial beings? "Spirits only are properly substance," we are told.[36] Edwards's answer was clear, and consistent with his idealism. All we actually meet when we speak of experiencing nature or matter are the deliverances of our senses and consciousness. Solidity, for example, is resistance to touch, and "this is all the knowledge we get of solidity by our senses." He was sure that was "all that we can get any other way."[37] What we obtain by perception is not solid matter, but an infinite resistance in space caused by "the immediate exercise of divine power."[38] All existence is perception and, as we previously saw, "what we call body is nothing but a particular mode of perception."[39] Unfortunately, Edwards did not spell out what made this mode of perception different from any other kind of perception. Nevertheless, bound by our perceptions, we have no grounds for inferring that behind these perceptions and our consciousness thereof there lurks material substance. As he had answered Hobbes's materialism, "No matter is, in the proper sense matter."[40] All we really know as matter are our perceptions and the ideas that spring from them. Therefore the world exists because it is perceived and thought.[41]

Edwards was quite aware that problems existed in his idealistic formulation. He admitted that in saying the material universe existed nowhere except in a mind "we have got to such a degree of strictness and abstraction that we must be exceedingly careful that we do not confound and lose ourselves by misapprehension." Of course, one does not intend to say that the whole world exists "in the narrow compass of a few inches of space" in the brain! One should rather remember that the human body and its brain exist only mentally and to talk of the placement of ideas in the brain is also to speak of place as an idea. Edwards then concluded that things were wherever they seem to be. Once having deposited all material things in the world of idea, he had no longer any need to distinguish reality from appearance, for appearance was reality. Like Berkeley, he thought he was giving a defense of "common sense" and not offering an esoteric philosophy.[42] After all, people do not find things disarranged in an idealistic philosophy. Everything is just as it was before in the vulgar way of looking at the world. The so-called physical world was still there, open to the inspection of science.[43] And in what looks like a stunning surrender of his whole philosophy, he maintained that it made no difference "whether we suppose the world only mental in our sense, or no."[44] In short, his philosophy had not changed a thing in the corporeal world, a conclusion that might well prompt the question as to what advantage there was in adopting it. With or without it, science could go on its way unaffected by metaphysical speculations. "Though we suppose that the existence of the whole material universe is absolutely dependent on idea, yet we may speak in the old way, and as properly and truly as ever."[45] One did not have to preface every reference to an object in the perceptible world with the words *idea of,* as for instance, the idea of a tree, a river, and so on. The common-sense way of speaking was sufficient.

But did these references to its not making a difference whether the world was idea or not and the ability to speak in the old way indicate that he had given up on his idealistic philosophy? Some commentators have decided that these words are evidence of the end of his fascination with idealism.[46] However, this may be too hasty a conclusion, since Edwards had produced, probably at Stockbridge in 1756 or 1757, a piece entitled "Notes on Knowledge and Existence" in which he affirmed his idealistic phenomenalism. It may be that after 1731, when he appears to have laid aside "The Mind," he turned to work on *The Freedom of the Will* and *Original Sin,* but the lure of idealism still had its hold upon him.[47]

In any case he was bothered about the brain when dealing in idealistic terms. In commenting on the way spiders perceive and feel, he mentioned in passing that their acts were "much after the same manner as the soul in the brain" acted.[48] In a different version he claimed that the seat of the soul was not in the brain "any otherwise than as to its immediate operation, and the immediate operation of things on it." Moreover—more strictly speaking, he thought—the soul was in the heart or affections. Since the senses of sight and hearing and the effects of thought and study are in the head, it was natural for men to place the brain and soul in the head.[49] But he was dissatisfied with this way of speaking of the soul and the brain, and admitted that he had spoken improperly. To speak "more strictly and abstractly," and presumably more accurately, he explained that what went on in the brain was the connection that the soul made between certain modes of its own ideas and the mental acts of the deity. This conviction indicated that to say the soul was in the brain meant that the brain itself was idea. So the brain as a physical organ did not exist, yet it was part of the corporeal world! Where then, in keeping with his idealistic phenomenology, is there a perception of the brain upon which the brain as idea exists? If we do not perceive our own brains at work, whether as physical or mental entities, how then is it proper to claim that the brain is an idea except by a subsuming of it under the general category of mentality, that is, that the whole world is mental?

Edwards revealed his acute discomfort with his own formulation by admitting, "we have got so far beyond those things for which language was chiefly contrived that unless we use extreme caution we cannot speak, except one speak exceeding unintelligibly, without literally contradicting ourselves."[50] The attempt to speak in the old way, with everything existing where it seemed to be, is incapable of expressing accurately what his mentalistic metaphysic demanded. The freight of physical connotations refused to fit neatly into the new way of speaking.

Edwards met an equally difficult problem when he set out to explain how sense organs, without being physical, gave rise to perception. If the sense organs have no existence but "what is conveyed into the mind by themselves," it would follow that "the organs of sense owe their existence to the organs of sense . . . being the causes or occasions of their own existence. . . ." But this made no sense to him, and he confessed that the inconsistency could not be explained or removed by reason.[51] How could the sense organs as part of the sensible world owe their existence to being perceived without affirming that they were logically prior to their being the cause of themselves? Some of our sense organs, such as the eye of the observer, are not perceived by the observer in the act of sensing, nor is the brain in the process of thinking available to the thinker. So baffled was Edwards by this conundrum that he asked how it could be that if sense organs exist only as ideas, their status could be rationally understood "when we have no idea of the mode of our organs, or the manner of external objects being applied to them."[52]

The problem essentially was that of affirming as real objects that by his own viewpoint were unperceived. Edwards confronted this issue in respect to atoms that were unperceived, but that, he had argued, made up the corporeal world. The way out of this dilemma was to affirm that although objects and atoms in the external world may not actually be perceived, they are not imperceptible in principle. Or even if no one perceives them, and they do not actually exist, "God supposes their existence in some mind," and causes all other ideas in us "as if they actually existed in that way," just as one may rightfully suppose that there were individual atoms in their primordial arrangement and motion, although unperceived.[53] They may not actually exist, but one supposed such entities to be necessary to round out a complete and determined system of the world. Hence these entities "must be supposed if the train of ideas be in the order and course" settled by the supreme mind.[54] And how does this tortured logic relieve Edwards's concern about sense organs? He moved to the notion that it was not proper to say that the dependence of our ideas of sensation upon the organs of the body is only the dependence of some of our ideas upon others. "For the organs of our bodies are not our ideas in any proper sense." Their existence may be mental, but not necessarily existing in our minds—they exist only as supposed. So in the last analysis, what we say about their supposed existence serves the same purpose as if they existed "in the manner vulgarly conceived."[55] It is not surprising then that Anderson concludes his analysis of Edwards on this point by saying, "there can be no doubt that he was genuinely perplexed by the theory."[56] Brains and sense organs had an embarrassing way of defying the strictures of idealistic phenomenology. Common sense as "vulgarly conceived" did not accord with what reason told him.

His difficulties with explaining the status of the brain and sense organs were typical of similar problems that proved recalcitrant. What, for example, was the perception upon which rested his idea of *externality?* He could not refuse the use of the term any more than he could deny that there was a "within" and a "without" to the body. As a perceiving being, he was sure these terms made sense, and therefore there was forced on him a distinction between what went on in the mind and to what these mental actions referred. The very idea of a corporeal body or world raised the same question. Bodies, thunder, rain, lightning, clouds, blood, fog, rainbows, plants, trees, and the like inhabited a realm that called for a distinction to be made—that called for an explanation that could not easily be interpreted as only the difference between ideas in the mind. Did not his reference to speaking properly in "the old way" belie the fact that his metaphysic

could not as such make sense of the appearances he actually encoun-
tered? Yet his general answer to externality at last depended less on
human perceptions than upon the postulate that God simply had so
managed things in that way; hence his conclusion: "In things that are
supposed to be without us, 'tis the determination, and fixed mode of
God's exciting ideas in us. So that truth in these things is an agreement of our ideas with that series in God. 'Tis existence and that is all
we can say."[57]
The relation between the human body and the soul was another
instance of a problem into which he was led by his idealism. If he had
given up his idealism late in life, when he penned his letter to the
trustees of Nassau Hall, we could understand his references to the
physical afflictions that debilitated his spiritual, mental, and intellectual endeavors. However, as previously pointed out, as late as 1756 or
1757 he was still writing in the vein of his idealistic metaphysic, and
no reference in the correspondence reflects anything other than an
acceptance of the reality of physical illness. What then was the relation of body to the soul or mind? He had, of course, given attention to
this problem. In one place he wrote, "all the way that the soul can
influence the body is only be emitting animal spirits from the brain."
On the other hand, "all the way that body has influence upon the soul
is by the influx of animal spirits to the brain or efflux from it."[58] We
have seen the difficulty Edwards had in treating the brain as idea
without perception, but what then are animal spirits? Are they physical or ideal entities? If physical, then it is difficult to see how the soul
could generate them, and if ideal, how the body could do so. The
passage that makes an effort to clarify the way animal spirits work, if
not their nature, reads like a physical description. He likened their
influence on the brain to that of a tube filled with water, which when
moved "never so little" at one end continues to the other end, that is,
to the brain.[59] But this is no solution to the nature of animal spirits,
for even if used as an analogy, its value depends on the acceptance of
the reality of the physical. And had he not instructed himself to
remember when he was to write about the human body to "let the
demonstration of the soul's being distinct from matter be inserted"?[60]
And matter does not think. Given his conception of matter as solid
impenetrable atoms, or extension, characterized by mobility and
subject to gravity, it is no surprise that he found the idea that matter's
incapacity for thought was scarcely worthy of dispute. Thought was
in no way dependent on the properties of matter and, in fact,
"thought could do as well without these properties," for perception,
the basis of thought, has no connection with solidity, motion, or
gravity. Yet he could not deny that God had so constituted affairs that

thinking could be added to matter in the sense that the two would be in the same place, although he doubted the propriety of saying that thought could be in a place. Nevertheless, thought is so connected with human bodies, or at least some parts thereof, that the two will be so "forever after the resurrection."[61]

So far the relation between the body or matter and the mind appeared as a kind of awkward juxtaposition of two alien entities. However, the union was not to be so considered. It was such that an alteration caused in the body was, he thought, probably due to action in the mind. And when the human body, especially the head, was impaired by disease, "almost every action causes a sensible alteration in the body."[62] It is noteworthy in these passages that although priority is given to the mind as the causal agent affecting the body, he did not cast the body in the familiar idealistic terms used elsewhere. In the *Religious Affections*, he stated the connection between body and mind in a more equitable fashion. By the laws of the union of soul and body, he affirmed, "there never is any case whatsoever" in which the vigorous exercise of the will or inclination of the soul does not have effect on the body. But by the same laws "the constitution of the body, and the motion of its fluids, may promote the exercise of the affections." Thus a kind of reciprocal interaction seemed established, but this two-way causal action is due only to God's constitution acting in such a way that some ideas follow from others as their cause, cause here being understood as fixity of connection.[63] In the case of affections, Edwards maintained that bodily actions were accompaniments to the mind's action, and were "in no way essential to them."[64] Yet, if the body promotes affections, although it is not their instigator, there is a closer alliance between matter and mind than Edwards seemed ready to admit. By the same token the relevant passages are best understood as emphasizing the reality of corporeal matter in spite of his repeated claims that the body, its organs, and the whole material universe existed nowhere except in the mind.[65] And to assert that the word *body* stood only for a "particular mode of perception" does not inform us as to what it is upon which perception fastens or serves, except by sleight of hand to turn matter into mind.

The relation between perceptions and material bodies presented a slightly different problem for Edwards when he spoke of atoms. In this case perceptions could not account for his commentaries on these aspects of the external world. Nothing he had observed, touched, or sensed as an inhabitant of the Valley or elsewhere permitted him to describe atoms or to position them in space. There was in his experience no basis to affirm them to be "truly in those places" wherever they seemed to be. Nor had the highly speculative theory of atoms, of which his scientific authorities spoke, provided a solid basis for his own hypothetical, a priori discussion of atoms. Unlike some of the scientists upon whom he depended, he had carried on no experiments from which to infer the reality or properties of atoms. If perception had provided no grounds for his belief in atoms, then he was entirely dependent upon those who had by experimentation come upon the theory of atoms as making up the material world. What they taught him was that atoms were literally solid, unbreakable, insensate pieces of matter, and from that basis his own speculations took off.[66] Perry Miller saw Edwards as moving sharply away from this naive view of atoms, but most of what Edwards wrote on them accepted what the scientists had given him, although he tried to explain their properties within his idealistic framework. According to Miller, Edwards, instead of following the lead offered by the science of his time, treated an atom as a concept, not as a particle of existing substance. This view on Edwards's part, Miller thought, "was useful in physics, not because it had spatial dimensions, but because it played only 'the role' of providing a point in which resistance could be concentrated."[67] But it is no less true that the properties that were given a mentalistic interpretation by Edwards were exactly those which the then-current science described. Solidity, impermeability, extension, and resistance were the starting points from which, according to Miller, Edwards developed the notion of atoms as models or concepts. Perhaps that was what Edwards intended, but nowhere in the passages on atoms did he explicitly affirm that atoms were mere concepts without exactly those properties with which science endowed them. If they were conceptual models, they were models fashioned upon qualities that no purely human ratiocination or perception either created or discerned. He talked in his hypothetically abstract manner of atoms as bodies touching, joining surfaces, colliding, or adhering. This certainly seems to be using with a vengeance the language of "the old way" of speaking. If an atom was a body of some kind, and no other sense can be made of it except that, then how could Edwards affirm that he found color to have "the chief share" in its nature? A body, wrote Edwards, is "nothing but color, together with some powers such as the power of resisting and motion etc. that wholly makes up what we call body."[68] But of what color or figure was an atom composed if it be counted a body? The senses afforded no basis upon which to answer the question. To be sure, Edwards defined figure as the "modification of solidity" or its extension,[69] but to what could he appeal in respect to color? If color was only in the mind and there was no perception of atoms to initiate the idea of color or colors in the mind, it would be logically improper to call an atom a body. But a body, according to Edwards's theory, also had the power of resistance and motion. Resistance is "the constant law or method" of God's exertion of power, and how, he asked, "is there any resistance except it be in some mind, in idea." Resistance as sheer physical power outside the mind makes no sense, because different resistances would be resisting each other, and that is "exceedingly ridiculous." However, it is easy, thought Edwards, to conceive of resistance as a mode of an idea. An "idea may be resisted—it may move, and stop, and rebound," but it is inconceivable that an unreal material power can do these things.[70] This kind of a priori reasoning, it may be noted, uses words such as *mind, stop,* and *rebound* as though they had meaning when abstracted from physical nature.

This kind of a priori reasoning does nothing to answer the basic question in Edwards's idealistic phenomenology, namely, how one can talk intelligibly about bodies and their properties where perception of these entities is entirely lacking. The words Edwards freely uses, such as *solidity, color, move, stop,* and *rebound* are vacuous without perception of something more substantial than the notion of the mind's "perceiving" its own perceptions. If atoms are unperceived, all ideas about them, no matter how sophisticated the reasoning may be, have no basis. It is little wonder then that Edwards had to have recourse to talking in the "old way" as though he were dealing directly with nature. But his final solution for the existence of atoms could be only to subsume them under the general explanation of the ideal existence of bodies as being "in God by way of his knowledge or consciousness of them."[71]

In spite of the problems of language and logic that Edwards had in trying to salvage the reality of bodies inclusive of atoms, his final defense was to assert that atoms were solid, impermeable, and so on, by virtue of the infinite power of an infinite being.[72] For example, finite physical power could neither be the cause of solidity nor the agency of its destruction. Therefore God, an ideal, spiritual being, had created and held in being atoms which, because they were rooted in Him, were as objective, though not materialistic, as God Himself. Atoms were not concepts subjectively devised by human minds as a kind of shorthand to make sense of the real world, but were objective, ideal, specific entities to which human minds had access, according to God's constitution of how human minds followed after God's thoughts.

To think God's thoughts after Him was not only to describe material phenomena in idealistic terms, but was also to ferret out the very principles or laws of God that brought order out of what otherwise would have been chaos. Science and philosophy were methods by which to enter into the causes or reasons why things were what they were, and how they moved and interacted. They were ways "to find out the proportion of God's acting."[73] Proportionality, along with such principles as harmony, symmetry, or agreement, was not so much a matter of perception, though it was that, as it was a deduction made on that basis which constituted a realm of universal principles that governed both the world of nature and the structure of all that could be called real. Thus he could write that ideas that depend on sensation or perception alone could "exceedingly clog the mind in searching into the innermost nature of things, and cast such a mist over things that there is need of a sharp sight to see clearly through."[74] To find these universal principles that frame and order nature was not a matter of observing natural phenomena as they were perceived, although Edwards granted that there might be "a foundation in nature for these abstract ideas we call universals." What was needed in addition was the recognition of how particular experiences of nature came to be called in different languages by the same or similar names, that is, to be understood as universal principles.[75] In working out this program of universals, Edwards argued that all universals "cannot be made up of ideas abstracted from particulars. . . ." For example, the ideas of color or sound could not be made up of ideas abstracted from particular colors or sounds because from simple ideas nothing can be abstracted. Universals were formed when the mind recognized that some of its ideas agree in a manner very different from all other ideas it also holds. The mind then ranks these ideas in order and calls them by the same name. So the soul or mind, by its own inherent powers that see similarity between certain ideas, which in turn excite other ideas, comes upon universals that are not merely arbitrary collections of sensed objects.[76] The mind is so constituted by God that here one thinks God's thoughts after Him. Hence in the case of proportionality, as with other universals, one rises above a sheer empiricism concerning the details of nature or other aspects of reality to a rationalism seated in the very structure of the mind. As the mind finds certain relations in nature and elsewhere, in different times and circumstances, it synthesizes into one principle the concept of proportionality. And to do so is to reflect upon real ideas as they exist in God's mind as He orders His world, inclusive of nature.

Although in Edwards's account of the method by which universals were arrived at, the mind's work was paramount, it cannot be totally denied that the ideas of proportionality, symmetry, harmony, agreement, and relationality owed much to his firsthand acquaintance with nature. It was these factors that seem from the very beginning of his thoughts about nature to have incited him to develop his theory concerning their ideal reality. And it was the excellence, beauty, and harmony of nature as he observed it that was at last to color and influence his ideas of the ethical and spiritual life. Both human and divine life were to be construed in terms drawn from them but that were not entirely dependent upon nature's patterns of harmony, proportion, agreement, and so forth, because these were not simply inventions of the human mind. They were structured ingredients in the very nature of reality as such.

The degree to which Edwards depended upon the reality of nature described in the "old way" can be seen in at least one aspect of his theology. He apparently accepted the reality of matter as it was presented in Scripture, and he gives no hint that the biblical writers' reference to earth or flesh was to be construed in purely mentalistic terms. But a central doctrine of orthodox Christianity that he found in Scripture would seem to demand that he surrender completely his philosophical position. That doctrine was the Incarnation.

In his "Essay on the Trinity" he had explained the generation of Christ as the replication of God in terms of his idealistic epistemology. God, he believed, had a perfect idea of Himself, and this knowledge was "something distinct from his meer direct existence." So God became His own object of knowledge in accordance with the metaphysical principle, elsewhere developed in Edwards's philosophical writings on "duplicity." This action of God was also in keeping with Edwards's conviction that nothing "should be from all eternity without its being conscious to itself that it was."[77] In knowing and being conscious of this idea of Himself, God generated repeatedly or continuously the Godhead, in which His perfections were represented and imaged. "Therefore as God with perfect clearness, fullness and strength, understands Himself, views His own essence . . . that idea which God hath of Himself is absolutely Himself." And this idea is the second person of the Trinity. "He is the eternal, necessary, perfect, substantial and personal idea which God hath of Himself. . . ." To make his point even clearer Edwards went on to claim that Christ was not only in the image of the Father, but was "the image itself in the most proper sense." By God's reflexive cognition of Himself the Son is begotten. The Son is the repetition of an idea of a knowledge that God has of Himself, and is thus an exact image of God. Knowledge is creative of that of which it claims knowledge.[78]

This whole discussion moves in the area of Edwards's metaphysical and epistemological thought without any reference to Christ's incarnation in flesh. However, in his "Observations concerning the Scripture Oeconomy of the Trinity," Edwards moved toward the doctrine of Incarnation when he referred to Christ as *the God-Man*.[79] And the usage of this term and its counterparts found fuller treatment in several of Edwards's sermons in which Christ's physical nature was made explicit. In the sermon on "The Excellency of Christ" we read that Christ took on "our nature" and that his condescension "appeared in the manner of his incarnation." Born in the womb of a poor virgin, he dwelt on earth in "mean outward circumstances." As subject to his mother and reputed father, he lived a life of poverty and humiliation. He suffered "pain in his body" and underwent "torment of body," and when he was killed, blood and water issued from his side.[80] Nothing could be clearer in the light of such passages than that Edwards needed to use the "old way" of speaking to make sense of the Incarnation. If matter or body was a mode of perception, what could fittingly be said about Christ's being in the flesh that made sense of the numerous biblical passages that accepted his physical nature? If Edwards had claimed that the idea of Christ only appeared in the idea of a body or flesh, he would have been moving in the direction of the Docetic heresy, and his orthodoxy forbade that conclusion. Without real material flesh, the Incarnation would have been nullified as the central tenet of the Christian religion.

Because Edwards never completed the system that would demonstrate "how all arts and sciences" when perfected would "issue in divinity, and coincide with it, and appear as parts of it," we cannot be sure that he would have been incapable of solving the problems that his scattered thoughts in "The Mind," the "Miscellanies," and his scientific writings and other pieces left unresolved. The outlines of the system can be discerned, but the fragments upon which we are dependent do not provide a final answer to the picture of nature he hoped to develop. The tension remains between his idealistic metaphysic and epistemology and the world of which he attempted to give a coherent account. What we have is Edwards's firm conviction on the one hand that the nearer things are to God, the more they are properly beings, and that spirits therefore "are much more properly beings, and more substantial, than bodies."[81] And this conviction accords well with his contention that things in nature were "made in analogy to spiritual things."[82] On the other hand, his thoughts on nature show a heavy dependence upon a nature that could be described in the old way, "whether we suppose the world only mental in our sense, or no." In this respect the "vulgar" or realistic way of talking about nature seems to have been justified. His discomfiture with the fitness of a language based upon this realistic conception of the world to describe spiritual things can be observed in his argument that the names of these spiritual things were all or mostly derived from the names given to sensible or corporeal entities. This, he held, was the only way of helping people understand what was meant, for spiritual things had an analogy to the names of sensible things.[83] A similar but more decisive emphasis was given to the importance of this-worldly realities in *The Nature of True Virtue*. In his description of how individuals can understand others only by "substituting ourselves in their place," he pointed out that "we never could have any notion what understanding or volition, love or hatred are, either in created spirits or in God, if we had never experienced" these attributes "in our own minds."[84] The reference, to be sure, speaks of mental or spiritual qualities rather than natural phenomena, but the import of the passage is that one passes intellectually not from spiritual things downward to qualities experienced in the world, but the reverse. Priority is given to what transpires in people within the commonplace world, as the sole means of understanding what occurs in the nontemporal world. In this respect it can be said that Edwards's thought took its start not from the spiritual world and then applied its ideas to worldly realities, but moved in the opposite direction as it did in respect to nature.

The traditional path of interpreting Edwards's thought moving, as it were, from the heights of spiritual and mental reality down to the everyday world of sensibility and common sense certainly has much support in his writing.[85] So Norman Fiering could contrast Francis Hutcheson and Edwards as to the contrary directions they took on the subject of their thoughts on beauty and morality. Hutcheson, thought Fiering, "began with certain formal physical relationships, such as symmetry and equality, and moved upward to moral relationships." Edwards, on the other hand, began with spiritual relationships and then descended to the material world.[86] Yet this is a great simplification of what Edwards in fact did, not only concerning beauty and morality, but also in respect to nature. It was nature that fixed Edwards's intuitive eye upon beauty and excellence, not pure ratiocination or revelation. Proportion, symmetry, agreement, and the whole conception of relationality was as much what Edwards claimed to see in nature as it was what he found in spiritual and moral relations at another level of his thought. It is this element in Edwards's thought that too often has led interpreters astray by their failure to recognize the essential part nature played in giving form and content to what Edwards talked about in idealistic terms. It was also a factor showing itself in the struggle Edwards himself had with constructing a language that could bear the weight simultaneously of his idealism and his realistic appraisal of what went on in the temporal world and nature.

Form 4 content to philosophical idealism

4

Nature and History in Symbolic Guise

ANDRÉ Gide once inquired, "What is more tiresome than the mania of certain writers who cannot see an object without thinking at once of another?" Some modern commentators on Edwards's typological writings would agree with the import of Gide's question. And Edwards himself gave a psychological reason as to why it was difficult to concentrate on one thing at a time. Because of the nature of the soul, he observed, "thinking of one thing, even against our will, excited the thought of other things that are like it."[1] Typology for Edwards was largely the working out of this insight. To look at or think about something in nature or in history was, as it were, to think immediately of that which it represented. The world became a typological one, where everything meant more than appeared at first inspection, where each idea dragged with it another idea presumed by him to be a higher truth.

In his "Note on Types" he explained that types were a certain sort of language in which God was wont to speak to us. Its idioms should be learned like any language by training and education and a careful comparison of things. Without such training and usage the interpretation of divine types would fail to express the beauty of the language and fall harshly on the ears of those who really understood the language.[2] Edwards at the same time was aware that taking the way of typology was not a popular device and would open him to ridicule and contempt. He confessed that he would be called "a man of very fruitful brain and copious fancy," but those who felt that way were welcome to their opinion. As for him, he defiantly answered, "I am not ashamed to own that I believe that the whole universe, heaven and earth, air and seas, and the divine constitution and history of the holy Scriptures, be full of images of divine things, as full as a language is of words. . . ."[3] And he was prepared to defend his ty-

73

pological procedure because it tended "to enlighten and illustrate, and to convey instruction with impressing conviction and pleasure, to help the memory." It was a method that had much in common with "man's delight in the imitative arts, in painting, poetry, fables, metaphysical language and dramatic performances."[4] When one considers the paucity of ornate, sensuous liturgical symbolism in Puritan worship and theology, then typology is perceived to have fed the faithful with dramatic symbolism that appealed to aesthetic as well as spiritual enjoyment. Stark, prosaic, theological dogma, and a life lived with the dullness of the daily routine amid commonplace objects, could both be invested with a vivacity and concrete relevance by which to follow the hazardous adventure of salvation. Against that background Perry Miller was not far off the mark when he observed that Edwards drew images from "the quality of life in the agrarian, hard-working, excitable Connecticut Valley of the mid-eighteenth century."[5]

In respect to the Bible, typology was a favorite tool by which to escape the jibes of skeptics and unbelievers who delighted in pointing to inconsistencies and contradictions among the various texts. Difficult passages whose meaning was not immediately evident could be transformed into more profound meanings by lifting them to the higher level of spiritual truth expressed in antitypes. Furthermore, when typological readings of the texts were subjected to careful theological and biblical norms, they could escape the exegetical dangers that came from the use of fantastic allegories or mere superficial resemblances between objects in nature or biblical texts and arbitrarily chosen spiritual meanings.[6] Typology was presumed to be a method, when guardedly employed, by which what was lacking in humanly devised symbols was made good by a system of spiritual images, types, and antitypes that were firmly embedded by God in the Scriptures and in creation. Its correct use, as Edwards put it in regard to the Old Testament, would reveal behind its historical events "in a mystery or parable, a glorious system of divine truth."[7]

In the development of his typology Edwards was treading a familiar path, one strewn with previous attempts to read human destiny by means of symbols believed to exist in nature, history, and the Bible. It was a path long used by Jewish and Christian exegetes.[8] Often the path was impeded by the brambles of ingenious reconstructions of biblical texts and farfetched analogies and metaphors drawn from nature. But typology came into its own with Edwards, according to the late Perry Miller, who persuaded many other scholars of American theology and literature to follow his lead in exalting the place of typology in Edwards's thought. Miller hailed Edwards's typology as a rhetorical form that unified science, history, and Scripture and whose theme carried one "to the very heart of Edwards' system." In this last judgment Miller was surely mistaken, for to many interpreters of Edwards his typology was more a pathetic alienation from than an indication of philosophical and theological acumen.[9] Miller also seems to have been carried away in his claim that Edwards had lifted nature "to a level of authority coequal with revelation" when Newton's world was looked on with a regenerate eye.[10] Scripture for Edwards was meant "to confirm the meaning of natural phenomena" rather than that they, as images, should confirm Scripture.[11] Unfortunately, this exaltation of the revelatory power of nature must be tempered by Edwards's own words. "The book of Scripture," he wrote, "is the interpreter of the book of nature" because it declared the spiritual mysteries signified and typified in the natural world.[12] Nevertheless Edwards, influenced especially by Locke and Newton, according to Miller, had rescued the interpretation of Scripture, nature, and history from the hands of those who, lacking his own philosophical sophistication, had wrought confusion in the art of exegesis.[13] It was against those who had brought typology into disrepute that Edwards had warned: "Persons ought to be exceeding careful in interpreting types that they don't give way to a wild fancy; not to fix an interpretation unless warranted by some hint in the New Testament of its being the true interpretation, or a lively figure and representation contained or warranted by an analogy to other types that one interprets on sure grounds."[14] It was a warning well urged, but one that we can see Edwards himself failed to heed. Allegorization and fantasy often obtruded into his typology. There is, for example, little to choose between Cotton Mather's melancholy musing on life while emptying his bladder as did a dog, and Edwards's finding dung a fit image of human corruption.[15] And Edwards's notion that "milk represents the Word of God from the breasts of the church" seems almost a replay of John Cotton's tract of 1646 entitled *Milk for Babes Drawn out of the Breasts of both Testaments*.[16] In such instances the superiority of Edwards's method over that employed by these Puritan worthies is scarcely discernible, contrary to Miller's unfavorable evaluation of Edwards's forerunners. Miller himself had to confess that some of Edwards's typological interpretations were "pedantries" and essentially quite traditional.[17]

Edwards, however, would not have regarded his typological venture in so dim a light. He was convinced that he was reading off from Scripture and worldly phenomena sublime truths concerning the goal of human existence. Typology had some resemblance to various art forms, but it was no mere artistic adornment loosely attached to

what he read in his Bible or saw round about him. In speaking of the
rays of the sun and beautiful colors that made the whole visible
creation "the shadow of being" and a representation of spiritual
things, he claimed that typology was no chance affair. "I don't pro-
pose this meerly as an hypothesis but as a part of divine truth
sufficiently and freely ascertained by the revelation God has made in
the Holy Scriptures."[18] After all, the Scriptures themselves contained
figurative language that called for interpretation, and surely the Bible should never be taken too lightly in these matters. "The histories
of Scripture," he thought, "are commonly read as if they were stories
written only to entertain men's fancies, and to while away their
leisure hours, when the infinitely great things contained or pointed at
in them are passed over and never taken notice of."[19] Typology was
for him the proper way by which to bring these great things to man's
attention.

The study of Edwards's typology has spawned a scholarly industry
in recent years. Fascination with tropes, metaphors, images, types,
and symbols has begotten a literature of its own that bids fair to
inundate American literary and theological studies. I do not wish to
venture too far into that sea of arcane discussion, but it may be well
to distinguish several ways in which Edwards used typology before
deploying some examples of his imagery. At the outset the distinction
between typology and other literary devices seems to have been
confused by Edwards himself. In his "Types of the Messiah" he referred to the fact that God in the Bible had used a variety of literary
forms along with types. Among these were what he called symbolical
representations, allegories, shadows, enigmatical speech, sim-
ilitudes, figures, and parables.[20] All of these seem to have been considered by him to be on the same footing as types, and therefore they
do not support the view that types stood out as a unique form of
rhetoric. But following the lead of those who best understand these
matters, I may distinguish three forms of what is loosely called
typology that appear to have been favored by Edwards.

Typology in the strict sense primarily refers to the understanding of
biblical texts by means of types and their corresponding antitypes. It
is characteristic of this typology that it employs types to exhibit and
reveal future events or, as in the case of Jesus Christ, a person. It is
essentially a symbolic way of reading history, or what is believed to
be actual history, in terms of antitypes, whose spiritual or ethical
meaning is projected by types in the literature itself. This usage is
best represented by "Types of the Messiah," "Notes on the Bible," and
the "History of Redemption." However, typology is not confined to
Scripture. Its use by Edwards extended to images or types in nature,

whether with nature directly experienced or as referred to in Scripture. "The wise man argues from an image in the natural world . . . ," he thought.[21] These images or types may be found scattered throughout Edwards's writings, but are best seen in a manuscript where Edwards collected them. Perry Miller published these under the title *Images or Shadows of Divine Things*. That Edwards counted nature as an important source of spiritual truths is sufficiently indicated by several of the titles considered for this collection, for example, "The Book of Nature and Common Providence" and "The Language and Lessons of Nature."[22] Generally, these types or images lacked the reference to the future, and dwelt more on the spiritual truths that could be descried in present circumstances. This fact moved Lowance to claim that Edwards only occasionally used "an earthly image to prefigure an event of the future. . . ."[23] Yet, an exception to this observation can be seen in Edwards's interpretation of the rainbow as in part a description of the future state of the church. Nevertheless, it could not be maintained as a criterion of a type that it refer only to the future. When Edwards wrote that none of the types of the Old Testament were more lively images of spiritual things than the growth of grass and vegetables, which were dependent on the sun and rain, he was pointing out that as natural phenomena depended on the elements, so also man depended on God for spiritual sustenance in present circumstances, not simply in the future.[24] It was his way of affirming that "there is an harmony between the methods of God's providence in [the] material and religious worlds."[25] A different meaning of typology can be seen when Edwards used biblical texts to illuminate past and present historical events. The "History of Redemption" and the apocalyptic writings are the main sources for this kind of typology. In particular he used biblical symbolism to explain the rise and subsequent ravages of the Roman Catholic Antichrist. For him the Book of Revelation was a virtual arsenal of types that, as for many Protestant theologians and biblical exegetes, served to defend Protestantism against the depredations and persecutions of the papacy. In these instances the past more than the present or future was the controlling focus of Edwards's typology.

Although it is wearisome to track down examples of his typology in each of these categories, it is helpful to give some examples of Edwards at work in each of them. Edwards, it need hardly be said, saw his whole world symbolically. It spoke to him of the highest truths and noblest beauties the Christian life should embody. But in his fierce realism about the human condition, its darker, uglier, and more depressing aspects had to have a major role. The higher spiritual

truths had their counterparts in the depths to which human nature
sank. Consequently, the story of images, types, and antitypes was not
an endless tale of ineffable beauties, but one that included accounts of
satanic powers, sin, suffering, condemnation, and divine punishment.

In the nature images this forbidding feature of the spiritual realm
was clearly spelled out. The birth of babies is one such example. As
they came into the world naked, filthy, bloody, and impotent, so in a
spiritual sense human beings, before grace does its work, bear the
taint of original sin and are spiritually naked and polluted.[26] The sun
is the image of Christ, whose beneficent light is shed on humanity,[27]
but its fierce heat stands for the wrath of the Lamb and "the ex-
tremity of the misery of the wicked."[28] Hills and mountains were
types of heaven, but in their valleys lies water that "commonly signifies misery, especially that which is occasioned by the wrath of
God." In short, water stands for hell, "a lake or gulf of misery and
wrath."[29] The flood was "the deluge of God's wrath,"[30] and the waters
over which the spirit brooded (Gen. 1:2) were identified with chaos as
well as a type of sin and misery.[31] Edwards seems to have had a
fixation on water as a sign of all that was evil and unruly. So when he
pondered the words of Revelation 21:1 that spoke of there being no
more sea, he dwelt on the fact that its waters were dangerous, uncer-
tain, unstable, never resting, the source of storms, clouds, and tem-
pests: "Water is the emblem of instability." But when the sea is no
more, so also will disappear all changes, dangers, doubts, difficulties,
and the afflictions of this world: "There shall be nothing but what is
firm and stable as the earth."[32] Edwards certainly found many images of spiritual beauty in nature, but this did not prevent him from
describing the world as "all over dirty," filled with that which "tends
to defile the soul" and pollutes human beings.[33] The human body is
filled with filthiness as the bowels are full of dung, representing the
filthiness of the human heart, and the "foldings and turnings in the
bowels" stand for "the great and manifold intricacies . . . and deceits
that are in the hearts" of sinful men.[34] This is typology near the end of
its tether, as far as spiritual edification is concerned.

Although Edwards stressed base, unattractive, and woeful aspects
of life, he could also portray the interplay between spiritual beauty
and the depressing side of human existence. "Roses grow upon
briars," he wrote, "which is to signify that all temporal sweets are
mixt with bitter," yet as the prickly bush grows, just so the rose,
"chief of flowers," appears in all its beauty and fragrance. And this
signifies that pure happiness, the crown of glory, can be achieved only
by bearing Christ's cross in mortification, self-denial, and labor. "The
end and crown of all is the beautifull and fragrant rose."[35] The

homely crudity of Edwards's talk of dung and the bowels is offset by his typological use of another part of the human body, the head. The head is the seat of the soul, which permeates the whole body by its power. So the Godhead dwells in Christ and in the whole body of believers, who participate in Christ as its head.[36] The world was "dirty all over" and from the perspective of eternity finally worthless, and become "too small a speck to be seen, i.e. it would still be less than nothing."[37] But in sharp contrast to this apocalyptic debasement of the world stood Edwards's intuitive sense of its beauty. The glory of the earth and the heavens bespoke in their images the higher, holy, spiritual realities. Even water, often used as an image of misery, sin, and condemnation, came to represent a divine process.[38] Water in the form of a river was the image of divine providence working its way through history against all obstacles. Many small streams and brooks, often running in different directions from the main course of the river, finally come together in the river and at last flow into the ocean. So obvious was the meaning of this extended image that Edwards casually remarked, "I need not run the parallel between this and the course of God's providence. . . ." Nevertheless, he proceeded to do so by pointing out that "all things shall have their final issue in God, the infinite, inextinguishable fountain whence all things came at first as all the rivers come from the sea and whither they all shall come at last."[39]

Edwards gloried in the "immense magnificence of the visible world in its inconceivable vastness" and "the uncomprehensible height of the heavens," all of which was an image "of the infinite magnificence, height and glory of God's work in the spiritual world. . . ."[40] Gravity holds the natural world together. By means of it bodies tend to each other for their mutual benefit, and this is a type of love or charity in the spiritual world.[41] Above all, Edwards found in heavenly bodies some of the most compelling images of the spiritual domain. Thus he could note that the different glory of the sun, moon, and stars represented the different glory of Christ and the glorified saints. The sun stood for Christ, and the moon for the prophets, apostles, and ministers of Christ.[42] As the sun sets in red, promising a fair day when next it rises, so "Christ the sun of righteousness set in blood," a type of his death, and rises to bring a "fair day" with blessedness and honor for himself and all those upon whom he shines.[43] The sun's light is not scattered by storms or high winds, so neither is Christ's heavenly light. "The light is of so pure and subtle a nature that that which is so gross as the wind can have no hold on it. Neither can things of the lower world dissipate Christ's light." These things, concluded Edwards, "are lively images of what is spiritual."[44]

Of the heavenly natural phenomena, the rainbow especially fascinated Edwards.[45] In part he was drawn to it by its inherent beauty, but also because of his scientific interest in Newton's optics, in which light rays were analyzed.[46] Above all, in an expanded interpretation of Genesis 9:12, he rang the changes on the spiritual significance of the colors and shape of the rainbow.

The rainbow was the token of God's covenant of grace, its light symbolizing his favor to his saints upon whom he shed hope, comfort, joy, excellence, and glory. Its beautiful colors represented the beauty and sweetness of the divine Spirit of love. Edwards then changed the figure by speaking of the light seen reflected in a cloud. That light symbolized the divine presence as manifested "in the flesh or in the human nature of Christ." The cloud protected men from the dazzling brightness of God's presence, which otherwise they could not endure. The cloud accommodated the divine perfections to "our manner of conception, so they were not as glaring as the sun itself, but sweet and inviting." The figure of the cloud again changes to become the source of water or rain that for the sake of men sheds down "its fatness, its nourishing, benign, refreshing influences on the earth" as did Christ by his dying for human beings. The drops of rain signified Christ's blood, his word, and "the blessed communications of his Spirit." Yet the cloud was but a vapor that vanishes. It was empty and unsubstantial, driven about by the wind, having no light of its own, being dark by its own nature. However, he did not follow through to explain the meaning of the clouds' evanescence or darkness. The raindrops were God's jewels and "as they are all in heaven, each one by its reflection, is a little star."[47] As such, they more fittingly represent the saints than do drops of dew. As raindrops come from heaven, so the saints were born from above, from the womb of the cloud that now stands for the church. Edwards then returned to consider the rainbow's colors. The rainbow contained different colors arranged in exact order "one above the other." This order showed the church to be made up of saints of different degrees, gifts, and offices, each in its own proper place contributing to the peculiar beauty of the whole.[48] As each drop of rain may be beautiful in itself, when united together the drops make up a whole that is even more beautiful.

Next, the total shape of the rainbow fixed Edwards's attention. As the rainbow rose from the earth toward heaven, so the saints from their first conversion "gradually climb the hill to the top," the bow of the rainbow being like the token of the covenant found in Jacob's ladder. The ascent is sharpest and most difficult at the beginning, but the ascent becomes easier the higher one climbs. On earth the rainbow is divided, its parts near the bottom being at a distance from each other, but at the summit they are united. This was a figure of the church. "So different parts of the church on earth may be divided" in respect to distance from each other, worship, opinions, and affections, but "will be united in heaven." But the observed rainbow is only half of the whole. "If completed [it] would be a perfect circle . . . fitly representing the most excellent order and perfect union that there shall be in the church of Christ." Fascinated by the notion of the perfect circle, Edwards placed Jesus Christ in the center of the circle, being reflected through the saints, each as a drop of water. A circle may be said to be full in the sense that its circumference is complete, but without content it is empty. So the church was an empty vessel until Christ filled it. Yet no matter how brightly each saint reflects the sun or becomes "a little image of the sun," no matter how extensive and beautiful the circle, still "the sun infinitely exceeds the whole in light, the whole reflects but little of the brightness of the fountain."[49] The shift from "sun" to "fountain" jars the literary symmetry of the passage, but it is to be remembered that the word *fountain* was a favorite term for Edwards's Neoplatonic thought by which to describe that which unstintingly pours forth its waters as does the sun its rays. It is a figure liberally used by Edwards in his treatise on God's last end in creation. In this passage as elsewhere, Edwards shifted the meaning of natural phenomena without any attempt to be consistent. A drop of rain could stand for Christ's blood or for the saints born from above. And many others of his images were bent to mean whatever it was he wanted to say at the time he penned these fragmentary examples of typology. In fact, there is an arbitrariness about his typology that belies Miller's claim that in Edwards's typology there was "vigorous correspondence" between the type and the antitype.[50] The types often seemed more like allegories, similes, and metaphors than evidence of a strict adherence to typological theory.

One example of Edwards's wrestling with the problem of accounting for the relation between natural phenomena and spiritual insight can be seen in his treatment of Revelation 21 : 6. In his scientific works he had said much about the size and shape of the world, the stars, and the heavens.[51] However, when the text referred to the passing away of the first heaven and earth and their replacement by a new heaven and earth, his science gave him trouble. He admitted the phrase "new heaven and earth" was "one of the most difficult parts of the Bible."[52] He knew this corporeal world would pass away,[53] but he was bothered by the realization that the new earth was to be the "habitation of bodies as well as souls." It was to be a place where the saints could "tread with their feet" and still have "an expanse over their heads." How could this be, if the saints were pure spirit without corporeal bodies, or the heavens above were understood as a spiritual reality? This new heaven and earth was to be a glorious place for the saints "removed at an immense distance from the solar system," but where then could it be? Of one thing at least Edwards was sure. This "last and everlasting abode of the church" was not to be confused with the visible globe, with its atmosphere renewed and purified. If that were the case, the same sun, moon, and stars now present would shine on a world merely refurbished. And that conclusion contradicted the text before him. Even the removal of these celestial bodies and their replacement by others "don't make a new heaven, any more than the changing of household goods makes a new house, when the same walls and roof etc. remain." Edwards had always maintained that God was the supreme spirit and the creator of this corporeal world, but here he burst out with: "Tis absurd to suppose, that 'tis a spiritual creating that brings into being a literal or corporeal heaven and earth." A spiritual being, it seems, could only create a spiritual world, "a new heaven and earth." So caught between his literalistic reading of the text and his scientific insights, on the one hand, and his search for a spiritual interpretation of the passage in question on the other, Edwards settled for a typological solution. The present earth and heaven were the type and shadow that will have vanished. "Then the antitype succeeds."[54] The whole exercise seems to have been an example of the conflict implicit in trying to speak in the "old way" and yet to do justice to the spiritual reality and biblical truth for which he was sure the actual world and heavens stood.

It is not surprising that much of his typology was based on inanimate nature. After all, much of his scientific work had been concerned with this form of nature, and it was inanimate nature that had fixed his attention from his youth in the Valley. He had gone to some lengths to show that dumb animals lacked rational faculties and were unfit for spiritual things.[55] But the sweep of his typology demanded that he pay attention to the animate world. In this respect, consciously or unconsciously, he moved into the centuries-old tradition by which animals were regarded as symbols of virtues, vices, or theological doctrines. Clement of Rome had seen the phoenix rising from its ashes as Christ rising from the grave. The pelican had been a symbol of Christ or the church, which fed its young by the blood drawn from its own breast. The elephant, for some unknown reason, was a symbol of chastity. An Egyptian bird was believed to tickle the lips of the crocodile, then enter its mouth and, after picking the crocodile's teeth, go on to tear up the animal's stomach and kill it. Such is the devastating effect of sin, which first lulls its victim to sleep and finally slays the unwary.[56] As late as the eighteenth century the dog symbolized man's baser parts such as gluttony, lust, coarse bodily functions, and general disruptiveness. However, a distinction was made between mastiffs, mongrels, curs that were lecherous, incestuous, filthy, snarling, angry, and sullen, and hounds that were noble, sagacious, generous, intelligent, faithful, and obedient. Dogs apparently differed in status as their owners differed in social status.[57]

How far Edwards's relative lack of attention to the animate world was influenced positively or negatively by this mixed tradition of allegory and typology it is impossible to tell. What is more certain is the fact that the breakthroughs concerning inanimate nature associated with Newton placed that realm in the forefront of scientific knowledge, while the biological sciences, although vigorously pursued, took a secondary position. Therefore it is not unreasonable to suppose that Edwards's typological use of animate nature was in many respects more fanciful and tended more to allegory because he knew less of biology than he did of the sciences associated with inanimate nature. As a result, the details of his observations about animal life gave way to more extravagant notions of the meaning of living forms then even those based on inanimate nature. Whereas his scientific knowledge of inanimate nature provided some minimal control over his typology, his lack of knowledge of animate nature allowed a more unrestrained symbolization. Even its relatively unpredictable nature was reduced to the mechanistic structure of laws of nature, as when he described the motion of animals.[58] And his description of the motion of blood, presumably the same in beasts as in humans, was regarded as following the laws of hydrostatics.[59] The bizarre imagery drawn from animate nature apparently owed little to any firsthand knowledge of this aspect of nature. Indeed, Edwards may properly be charged with failure to obey his own warning "to observe the danger of being led by fancy."[60]

In the main Edwards used the animate world as containing types of evil and satanic forces. Yet there are several exceptions. The silkworm was "a remarkable type of Christ."[61] Like the silkworm, the bee was also designed as a type of Christ, "who having spent his life gathering . . . and laying up in store the most delicious food, having completed his work, is killed and by his death yields all his stores for the refreshment and delight of his murderers."[62] Some birds represent the inhabitants of heaven, for they occupy the highest world. With their glorious colors, power of flight, and music sweetly praising their creator, they are above the beasts and fishes. "The fishes in the waters under the earth represent those in hell, as also do whales and sea monsters."[63] The bird symbolism was carried on by recognizing that as the crowing of the cock awakened men from sleep, so also the glorious day of the church was to be heralded by ministers preaching the Gospel, as did also the singing of birds in the spring.[64] Christ shelters his saints that he has brought forth and fed, as does a parent bird.[65]

The picture changes when Edwards speaks of snakes and spiders. Serpents that charm birds and then eat them, and spiders that suck the blood of ensnared flies are "lively representations of the Devil's catching souls by his temptation."[66] As serpents swallow by degrees prey that is too large for them, so Satan destroys multitudes of men that have had so good an education or so much conviction and light and common grace that they are too big to be swallowed at once.[67] Poisonous and hurtful animals and insects such as serpents and spiders hide and lurk in secret places, and "herein they are types of devils and dupes of men."[68] But the devils will torment each other on judgment day, as spiders devour each other when shut up together.[69] Certain birds, although they inhabit the heavens, are types of evil. Ravens, for example, which feast on carrion, are "remarkable types of devils who with delight prey upon the souls of the dead."[70] The screaming, shrieking, and dolorous sounds of devils put Edwards in mind of those devils who, dwelling in darkness like the dragons in Micah 1 : 8, will wail in the morning.[71] Just as beasts of prey like lions range abroad in the night to destroy and devour, so in the dark time in the moral world devils seek whom they may devour, but when the sun of righteousness rises, they are to be confined to the bottomless pit.[72] Those who fall prey to the "lion, tyger or crocodile" will be filled with infinite horror and amazement at the "terribleness" of these beasts.[73] The crocodile egg is no bigger than a goose egg, but the crocodile from that egg becomes a great destructive creature. "So sin is comparatively easily crushed in the egg . . . but if let alone . . . how great and strong, terrible and destructive does it become and hard to kill, and grows as long as it lives."[74] Beasts go about with their heads bent to the ground to eat, whereas men's heads are toward heaven, thus showing that "the highest good of the beasts is earthly, but that man's proper happiness is heavenly."[75]

Numerous other animals were typified. The ass, which is the dullest of animals, has the fattest heart, so in Scripture it is said, "Go make their hearts fat, i.e. gross and dull." The "ass fish" with its heart in its belly, is a fit emblem of a sensual epicure.[76] Foxes are types of devils and enemies of the church.[77] The hog is an image of an earthly, carnal man, and is fed only to be slaughtered.[78] And the lowly mole that does not open its eyes until it is dead may be taken as the sinner, who after life is over, becomes aware of his true condition.[79]

On the other hand, animals could represent spiritual virtues. Thus the animals gathered in the ark were "a lively image of that gathering together of the elect from the four winds, from one end of heaven to the other."[80] In one of his sermons Edwards held Christ to be both the Lion, the Lion of Judah signified by Jacob's blessing, and the Lamb. Unlike the lion that devours, the lamb was the one slain. While the lion excels in strength and in the majesty of its voice, the lamb excels in meekness and patience, and providing food and clothing for man. Edwards did not make clear how these incompatible attributes came together in the person of Christ, but he assumed on biblical grounds that they did.[81]

Typology in the stricter literary sense deals with the types, anti-types, and history found in Scripture. Especially significant in this model of typology was the emphasis Edwards laid on actual histor-ical fact as the basis of his typology. So great was his confidence in the historical trustworthiness of the Bible that he went to great lengths to describe how Moses had written the Pentateuch. Moses, he thought, had been commanded to write "histories of the acts of the Lord," giving the actual historical context in which these acts took place lest anything be forgotten by future generations. The accounts of the travels of the children of Israel, for example, were not left to tradition or oral transmission. Like all other events, the story was transmitted by the written record.[82] Specific places were named whose impor-tance was explained.[83] And this history was intended not only to prompt the memory, but also to serve as a means of enforcing the commands and prophecies associated with the law. Such history, Edwards wrote, "was introductory, a concomitant, or confirmatory to the precepts, and threatenings, and promises that follows, and of this nature is all the history of the Pentateuch." Without it the law could not be understood.[84] The various accounts of events, places, and persons were all consistent with each other, giving evidence that Moses was presenting a unified historical account and not one patched together at some later date by another hand.[85] So well known was the writing of history by the Jews that other ancient nations imitated them by also keeping records.[86] And from these pagan and secular sources Edwards sought corroboration for the trustworthiness of biblical history.[87] So on what he regarded as a solid basis of accurate information, Edwards reared his typology, always sure it was founded in the data of actualities, not on a world of images or shadows. And it is not too much to claim that this in-sistence upon the actualities of biblical history saved nature, when referred to in the texts, from the fate of becoming an illusion, the dangerous direction toward which his idealistic phenomenology tended.

In the work entitled "Types of the Messiah" Edwards organized the antitypical meaning of much of the Old Testament around types that foreshadowed the future actions of Christ. By their actions, achievements, and words, the central figures of Jewish religious history turned out to be prefigurements of the Messiah. The list of types ran from Noah and Moses through Joseph, Deborah, Gideon, Samson, Daniel, and Solomon. Each of these in his or her respective way was a redeemer, victor over enemies, or a just ruler over periods of peace, rejoicing, and prosperity, and one at least, Solomon, was called a son of God.[88] No less significant were the events and practices of the Jews that pointed to what would happen in the messianic days. The redemption of the Jews from Egypt and many lesser redemptions and deliverances signified the coming great salvation of God's people.[89] Or as Edwards put it, "The ancient state of things amongst the Jews was all typical of the Messiah."[90]

Among those things upon which he dwelt was the importance of laws that disciplined sin, and legal prescriptions that guided one toward the messianic age. Above all, sacrifices foretold the sacrifice of Christ.[91] The "Notes on the Bible" took up similar themes such as that of the tribulation of the Jews that forecast what Christians would endure.[92] In the practice of Jewish circumcision Edwards discovered a symbol of the mortification and denial of the sin of lust. In cutting off a portion of the "instrument of generation" the natural corruption that had been passed on by the parents of mankind was typified.[93] This symbolism was also founded on an actual practice, though Edwards gave it his peculiar interpretation. Less obviously based on historical fact was his detailed description of how the world was populated by the tribes descended from the sons of Noah.[94] Thereby he introduced a historical gloss on events for which no scriptural evidence existed. So, as he had announced in "Types of the Messiah," events were historical fact, bearing out his claim that the Old Testament was from beginning to end a depository of typical things under which history was hid, "a glorious system of divine truth."[95]

In his letter to the trustees of Nassau Hall, among other personal reasons for his reluctance to accept its presidency, Edwards mentioned his intention to complete "a great work, which I call a History of the Work of Redemption." This was a piece he had begun earlier in his career in sermons preached in 1739. It was to be "a body of divinity in an entire new method, being thrown into the form of history. . . ." Apparently he came to regard this as a detailed and unified treatise describing by typology but based on history how God through Christ had been carrying out his redemptive work in successive historical periods. The work was projected against the background of the three worlds of heaven, earth, and hell, "so far as the

Scriptures give any light."[96] To execute this purpose Edwards found it necessary to speak of events that occured in heaven prior to the creation, of which the Bible gave no account. Among these events were the creation of the Trinity, the creation of the church, and the existence of Christ.[97] Much of the history dwelt upon the role of Satan in his attempt to frustrate God's plan. If Christ had not intervened, Adam and Eve would have been immediately seized by the devil, and on through the history of humanity the battle had gone on. It was especially evident in the rise of the Antichrist in Roman Catholicism. One startling item concerning Satan was omitted from the "History." In the first corollary to Miscellany 980, a strange piece of typology concerning affairs in heaven shows up. There Edwards wrote "Hence learn that Satan before his fall was the Messiah or X or as anointed." Thus what seemed to be a factual statement was converted into typology in Corollary 5 of the same entry. "Lucifer in having the excellency of all those glorious things that were about him all summ'd up in him he was a type of X. . . ."[98] But of all these pre-creation days there is no account in scripture, whereas events to occur in the future messianic time of Christ's triumph could at least be justifiably based on biblical prophecy.

In what guise did nature appear in his "History"? In many passages Edwards had recorded the beauty and order of nature, animate and inanimate. However, in this work he spoke of the ruin brought on physical bodies as well as souls. In the *Religious Affections*, as we have seen, he offered the opinion that Satan could excite thoughts and effects in the soul only "by causing some motion or alteration in something which appertains to the body." Only by means of the body could the devil affect the soul.[99] This was precisely how sin had captured humanity, but in the culmination of redemption "all the bodies of the elect are to be saved as well as their souls."[100] The end days Edwards described in what certainly are intended to be physical terms. Then temporal prosperity will flourish and there will be "a tendency to health and long life." And with ease, quietness, pleasantness, and cheerfulness of mind there would be a "great increase of children."[101] The Fall, however, had done more than wreck human life. It had affected the divinely ordered structure of nature as a whole. "The world was ruined, as to man, as effectually as if it had been reduced to chaos again; all heaven and earth was overthrown."[102] But as the "Miscellanies" tell us, there will be no salvation for nature as for the elect.[103] The impenitent "shall be consumed with this accursed world after the day of judgment, while Christ and his church shall triumphantly and gloriously ascend to heaven."[104] These passages affirm that although the world of nature will finally be destroyed, the human bodies of the elect, a part of nature, will be preserved. So the ambiguity concerning nature in Edwards's thought remains. Were bodies only images or shadows, or were they independently substantial entities? Was the world of nature apart from man dependent for its existence upon the ideas in human and divine minds that were to disappear when God was no longer creating it by his knowledge?[105]

In his philosophical writings Edwards admitted that it made little difference whether one regarded the world from the standpoint of his immaterialist philosophy or in some other way. All things would still be where they seemed to be. So science could be pursued in any case, and things could be spoken of in "the old way," that is, with common-sense realism.[106] In this way he had opened the way to treating nature as something other than a purely ideal construction or, as previously stated, as an inferior actuality. In his biblical typology he accepted the position that God used actually existing things to prefigure or describe the course of divine salvation. Was the import of Edwards typology a repudiation of the mentalistic metaphysic that the passage in "The Mind" had also implied? With all he had written in defense of immaterialism and his obvious emphasis on the spiritual or ideal world, it would be strange to find Edwards embracing a view that contradicted that position. But how far is he to be held responsible for maintaining a consistency of viewpoint between his philosophy and his biblical typology? It has been suggested that when he went to Northampton he gave up his philosophical work in favor of his pastoral and preaching duties. His typological writings then could be considered an entirely new start, which stressed theological matters as they pertained to his role as a clergyman rather than to his philosophical position. Yet some continuity existed between these two phases of his career, as the Stockbridge treatises show. A modern author, Bruce Kuklick, who noted Edwards's surrender of his philosophical work when he assumed his duties as pastor, has also claimed that "the later writings were elaborate but still founded on the earlier idealism."[107] This continuity between his philosophy and theology is supported by the piece previously mentioned, which was probably written at Stockbridge in 1756 or 1757. There he still affirmed the idealistic phenomenalism he had developed earlier.[108] If this reading of his intellectual career be accepted, then he is to be held responsible for the contradiction between the speculations in "The Mind" and his acceptance of the actualities he found in Scripture as the basis of his typology, actualities that included references to nature.

Over and above the problem of the metaphysical status of nature in the typological writings was the religious and ethical status Edwards granted to nature in these works. Metaphysically, nature, whether actual or as idea, was an inferior realm, and accordingly was often spoken of as debased in a religious sense. Yet that same nature, as an image of divine things, filled with extraordinary beauties, pointed to spiritual beauties and truth. On the one hand, nature represented all that was temporary, inadequate in itself and even corrupt, while on the other it was a reflection of all that was noble, inspiring, and divine. In the former sense Edwards's typology demeaned nature and by some of the images and types he drew from it, worked against the reigning scientific interest in it, in which he himself participated. In the theological and ethical sense, by finding edifying symbolism in nature, he debased and yet elevated it at the same time. On the whole, nature when treated typologically was degraded and distorted to serve the higher purposes of Edwards's endeavor to place the religious life on a plane above anything that smacked of materialism, lest the divine glory be contaminated by things of this lower world. Yet along the way Edwards had left hints of the actuality of nature that did not correspond to his philosophical idealism. He could have retained, as others did in his day, a realism about nature's independent metaphysical status as created by God, and at the same time found a religious symbolism that fed human spiritual aspirations. But the union between his philosophical idealism and religious sensibilities triumphed over any tendency to develop the incipient realism detectable in his struggles with the ambiguities of nature in "The Mind" and frankly acknowledged in the historical basis of his biblical typology.

The typology of nature customarily referred to spiritual truths that could be appreciated in the present. The typology of scripture usually referred to future and apocalyptic matters. But contained within it was a third kind of typology that was used to interpret past and present events. The words used were prophetic, but they were illuminative of what had happened in history, rather than events yet to come. This typology had an obvious apologetic purpose that concentrated on the defense of Protestantism by reading from the texts the evils let loose in the world by Satan's use of Roman Catholicism. Its tone was vindictive, expressing the hatred of Papistry common to Protestant reformers and theologians as they dwelt on the unspeakable horrors that Catholicism had visited upon innocent Protestants who held to the true faith. Wherever he could, Edwards traced in scripture the history of this sad story.

In his "Notes on the Bible" (Genesis 6:4) he found reference to the sons of God marrying the daughters of men and bringing forth monsters. This was a clear indication that the conjoining of holy things with wicked ones led to the description of Rome as "that monstrous beast."[109] The cleansing of the temple as a den of thieves (Matthew 21 : 12 ff.) was not only an example of Christ's chastising the apostate Jewish church, but the Jewish church was "in many ways an image of the apostate Christian church, or rather the anti-Christian church. . . ."[110] False prophets and false Christs were obvious types of the Great Antichrist, the Pope, and his clergy.[111] And in his "History of Redemption" Edwards offered an extended description of the rise of the Antichrist.[112]

The book of Revelation, to which he devoted an entire commentary, with its references to beasts and what Edwards took to be allusions to historical events, was filled with types condemning Catholicism and occasionally Anglicanism. The second chapter of Revelation concerning the church at Ephesus was particularly adapted to the state of Christians at the time of the Reformation. Then, as Edwards would have it, Christians began "to discover popish lies, cheats, impostures, and found out the falseness of the pretenses of the Romish clergy to apostolic power and succession and infallibility and power of working miracles. . . ." And the passage was also adapted to the case of the dissenters in England who cast off prelacy and rejected pretended divine right, apostolic succession, and the power of those who would make laws binding people's consciences. The church at Smyrna was related to the Reformed Church, which would have nothing to do with the synagogue of Satan, obviously the church of Rome. The church of England was likened to the church at Pergamum, which dwelt "even where Satan's seat is."[113]

Verse after verse yielded what Edwards apparently believed to be evidence of the work of Satan through the agency of Catholicism. Animals were types of analogies. The beast that was like a leopard, that is, "spotted and gay," denoted the "foolish gaiety" of its worship. Its feet, like those of a bear that hugged its victims to death, typified "the hypocrisy of their proceedings." The mouth,like that of the lion, signified the covetousness with which the Catholic Church devoured man's substance and estates.[114] The words "that no man should either buy or sell" was a reference to the anathema pronounced by the Lateran Council against the Waldensians, or Pope Martin the Fifth's bull prohibiting Roman Catholics from allowing heretics to dwell, do business, or fill any civil offices in their countries.[115] The woman in the wilderness, who fell prey to the dragon, stood for the Waldensians and Albigensians, who underwent dreadful persecution.[116] The water image, which had undergone many changes of meaning, once more was put to use, this time against Catholicism.

"Waters and rivers are in scripture language put for all temporal supplies." On this basis the Euphrates River stood for the supplies and wealth that nourished Babylon, the Romish church. And in still another reading, the water meant papal revenue, drawn off from many countries, which like streams converge in the "waters of a mighty river" that supports the kings of the spiritual Babylon.[117] Coming closer to his own period in history, Edwards found attempts to overthrow Protestantism had been halted in England by William and Mary.[118]

Not content with typological interpretations of Scripture on Catholicism, Edwards kept accounts of events in his own day that he believed fulfilled the meaning of the sixth vial mentioned in the book of Revelation. One account was a series of news items taken from the newspapers that described events to the disadvantage of Catholic religious and political interests. It was largely made up of stories or brief comments concerning the victories of English arms against French and Spanish forces or calamities that had befallen such Catholic centers as Spain, Italy, Austria, Portugal, or France. Another account recited events that showed Christianity was flourishing not only in America, but in Switzerland, Russia, England, Ireland, Scotland, Asia, France, Germany, and Holland. "Mohamitans" and Jews were being converted, and prominent individuals as well as native Americans were falling under the sway of evangelical Christianity. These bits of information, garnered from approximately 1747 to 1755, may not, strictly speaking, be typological, if that term is used prophetically to denote events yet to come. But they were contemporary confirmations of scriptural prophecy. One did not have to wait for future vindication of biblical prophecy or typology. The vindication was obvious in present events open to the observation of any who took the pains to look at them. All that was necessary to establish the truth of Scripture on a worldly plane was to regard these contemporary events from the standpoint of Scripture.

Metaphysically, the whole typological project seems to have been based on Edwards's two-world theory. His idealistic phenomenology told him there was both an actual, corporeal world and a superior world of pure spiritual ideality that lay beyond the world of sense and historical fact. Had he not laid it down as an accepted truth that the whole system of created beings, both nature and history, was to be conceived as divided into two parts, the typical and the antitypical worlds? The former he maintained was inferior, carnal, external, transitory, inchoate, imperfect, and subservient to the superior antitypical, more spiritual, perfect, and durable world that was the end and consummation of the typical world. "Thus," he explained, "the material and natural world is typical of the moral, spiritual and intelligent worlds, or the city of God." And he made it clear that this distinction applied not only to nature or things spoken of in the Bible, but to secular affairs as well.[119] This two-world theory would seem to accord with his idealistic metaphysic, wherein reality was idea and therefore akin to the spiritual realm, and matter was reduced to a form of human or divine perception.

revision

However, Edwards did not make this two-world theory work consistently. In his biblical typology he did not deny the actuality of persons, events, or natural objects. He gave no hint that these were ideas constructed by the mind. Rather, as he put it, God made use of things "that had an actual existence to typify them."[120] This reference to actual existence puts in doubt his notion that reality was purely ideal. It is a term that can scarcely be interpreted as equivalent to ideal reality. Rather at this point Edwards was in agreement with modern interpreters of typology who remind us that "to the mind of the New Testament writers the prophetic foreshadowings that they discerned in the history of Israel could have no importance if the events had not occurred in actual fact."[121] Accordingly, what he read in Scripture was literally valid historical information about real persons, institutions, events, and natural objects. These things could be spoken of in the old way without any reference to ideal reality.

Yet, while clinging to his two-world theory, it was necessary to provide some link between the two. That link was analogy, which as previously indicated was embedded in the very structure of God's creation. Hence, in spite of other disagreements with George Turnbull, Edwards avidly seized upon that writer's opinion that all language was derivative from sensible objects or their properties and effects. "No words," Turnbull claimed, "can express moral ideas but so far as there is such an analogy betwixt the natural and moral world. . . ."[122] That was language that nicely fitted the answer to Edwards's rhetorical question when he asked, "is it not natural to suppose that the corporeal and visible world should be designedly made and constituted in analogy to the more spiritual, noble and real world?"[123]

However, in what metaphysical sense could Edwards maintain that there was an analogy between the two worlds without admitting that the lower world had actual being apart from human perceptions? Logically, since the corporeal, sensible world was made up of images and shadows, and the superior "real" world was also constituted of pure ideas, the two worlds coalesced into one mental reality. How then could there be an analogy between the two worlds except as some ideas resembled other ideas? But then the perceived world would lose all that identified it as corporeal and external. It would not be what it seems to be. Analogy, however, depends not only on similarity between two or more entities, but upon an actual metaphysical difference or polarity lest, as Edwards said, "twoness (duality) is destroyed and they become one."[124] Without that polarity analogical reasoning is bereft of one of its principal conditions. Nor does it alleviate Edwards's predicament in respect to analogy to claim that the two worlds are describable in opposing terms, the one being transitory, the other stable and permanent, since in both cases, consistently with his idealistic phenomenalism, the two worlds enjoy the same metaphysical and epistemological status. Both are products of the mind, which is to say that duality is lost and the two become one in spite of whatever other differentiating attributes each has. In his biblical typology, but much less so in his nature typology, Edwards had guarded against this particular danger by affirming that God had used things that actually existed, and he simply accepted it as a fact that there was an analogy between the actual world and the world of antitypes.

The fact that God had created the lower world in analogy to the superior was still basic to the whole typological enterprise. The two worlds were linked to make up one world under God. There had to be a relation then to make this possible, and analogy was one formulation of the relation. "Two beings can agree one with another in nothing else but relation. . . ."[125] And Edwards's speculations concerning the structure of the world had already put into the foreground this principle of relationality, which now could be employed to explain the rational grounds for analogy.

Several metaphysical choices lay before Edwards in explaining the way the world, whether ideal or physical, was constructed. On the one hand, he could have considered each entity, whatever its content, as absolutely self-identical, lacking relations with every other entity. By definition each entity would then have been totally independent of every other. This would have been the extreme of sheer atomicity. But the adoption of this position would have brought his philosophy to an end before it got started. He would have been announcing a metaphysical and scientific tautology that flew in the face of all he had learned about gravity and the "mutual tendency of all bodies to each other."[126] On the other hand, by his scientific insight and aesthetic sensibility, he emphasized the supreme principle of reciprocal or mutual relationality. But even that alternative, if not carefully used, would have reduced any particular entity or body to a sum of relations without any unique essence of its own. To do so would have been to envision a world where nothing was itself or was located where it seemed to be. The world would have been made up of concatenations of relations wherein no beings would be fixed and determined to be what in fact they were. This was too high a price to pay for magnifying the role of relationality. Instead Edwards saw the world as one in which God created specific entities, ranging from atoms and objects to minds, and placed them where He pleased in space and time, subject to His law. Edwards could then explain how "the laws of nature take place alike" and "how it is laws that constitute all permanent being in created things, both corporeal and spiritual."[127] Each entity possessed its own unique properties and produced its own special effects, but by the principle of relationality and his laws, God had created the whole system, natural and spiritual, as organically and harmoniously united. No one entity within the system existed, as it were, in a vacuum. All was related, and the bond was forged by which one could confidently and reasonably pass, by analogy or typology, from the corporeal to the spiritual world. As relationality operated within the natural and the spiritual worlds, so also it operated to bind together the two worlds. Spiritual truths therefore could be read off from nature and Scripture as they could be from history.

This metaphysical linkage between the two worlds can be construed as a method of explaining how the truths of nature and Scripture constituted a unity. As the external nature was made a unity by the laws of science, so also the Scriptures constituted a unity by their history, the central purpose of which was to exhibit God's wisdom and power in salvation. From beginning to end, in every part, the Bible was to be read as a seamless story wherein people, events, institutions, and natural objects were actual and at the same time could serve as types foreshadowing or describing anti-types in the spiritual world. The story told by actual history was itself a unified one, forming the typological basis for what Edwards deemed to be an even more profound, unified account opened to human consciousness by the correct interpretation of antitypes. Similarly to read nature aright as images or representations of spiritual realities was to continue the same story whereof Scripture spoke, but different only by focusing upon it from a different metaphysical point and by a slightly different method. In his "History of Redemption" Edwards put the entire story together when he called the story of redemption all "one work, one design." The various dispensations or works that belonged to redemption, he said, "are but the several parts of one scheme."[128] Thus with complete confidence Edwards could conclude that "there is an excellent agreement between these things," that is, shadows or images in nature, "and the holy Scripture."[129]

Metaphysical argument provided a reasonable basis for the agreement between the testimony of nature and Scripture. However, by its inevitably abstract nature it could not yield the religious meaning Edwards wanted to attribute to images and types. The unity of meaning he discerned in both nature and Scripture drew upon his Calvinistic perspective. Scripture, the interpreter of nature, was read by him through the lens of a Calvinist theology that gave specific religious meaning to what otherwise would have been mere philosophical abstractions. Certainly interpretations of the images and types did not lie exposed on the surface of either nature or the pages of the Bible. These items were to be fashioned by Edwards into a unity of meaning by an imagination trained in and imbued with what he took to be orthodox Calvinist doctrine. Whatever were the details of these interpretations and in spite of their logical inconsistencies, together they made up a story of redemption for the elect and damnation for the nonelect. But the arbitrariness with which he treated the religious meaning of nature and Scripture was being severely questioned even in his own day, and in a later time scholars with more sophisticated theological and biblical methods created from the same texts a far different account from that of Edwards. However, Edwards's confidence in the truth of his variant form of Calvinism guaranteed that nature and Scripture would speak with one voice of the sovereign God's dealings with His world. Typology was the rhetorical means by which that voice could be heard and understood.

Typology certainly was intended by Edwards to be religiously edifying, but was not something more needed to appropriate and appreciate what it offered? Much has been written about Edwards's use of the term *a new spiritual sense,* and it has been assumed that such a sense was required for truly understanding and "closing with" God's revelation in nature and the Bible. By definition, those who failed to do so obviously did not possess this new sense, which was a gift of God. To them neither nature nor Scripture opened its divine treasures. One modern author has been so thoroughly convinced of this position that he claimed "for Edwards nature's revelation was possible only for an elect and regenerate sensibility."[130]

However, it may be asked to what audience were his typological writings addressed? On the face of it Edwards intended these writings to edify elect and nonelect alike. Any reasonable person, he supposed, could follow his philosophical speculations in support of the use of analogy, upon which his typology depended. And similarly nowhere did he assume that a regenerate sense was necessary for understanding the meanings he ascribed to nature's images or biblical types and antitypes. And certainly his third type of typology did not call for a new sense to appreciate its references to history. Natural men may have a sense of the natural perfection of God, he admitted, but he maintained that saints alone recognized the beauties of these attributes.[131] So to achieve this higher sense God had given to some persons a "kind of taste," an intuitive sense of the true spiritual and holy beauty of divine things, having more or less the Spirit of God dwelling in them.[132] Clearly for Edwards this new sense was of crucial importance, for it distinguished between the elect and the nonelect.

Those scholars who have emphasized the new sense have often appealed to Locke's "stress on sensation and direct experience as the basis of all knowledge" as the source of Edwards's idea of the new sense. But there are those who deny or reduce the significance of Locke's influence. Paul Helm noted that Edwards used Lockean empiricism as a model for religious experience and "nothing more." Rather, Edwards used "the language of the 'new way of ideas,'" such as sense and simple idea, as an attempt "to highlight what in his view was the peculiar character of religious experience—its non-natural character."[133] And Norman Fiering, as was noted, even more directly scouts the notion of Locke's influence by arguing that Edwards's spiritual sense has little resemblance to anything in Locke, and he concludes that Locke would have dismissed Edwards's notion of a special sensation of divine things as "enthusiastick" nonsense.[134] It appears that Edwards's sense of the heart owed more to his Calvinist and Puritan heritage than it did to Locke, with whom he disagreed quite as often as he agreed, his conception of human self-identity being one outstanding example.[135]

Even if the new sense marked the line between the elect and nonelect, Edwards was always careful not to make that line too clear, in spite of the difficulties in which he was entangled that led to his dismissal from the Northampton pulpit. He did not flinch from distinguishing the two kinds of human beings, but he knew that it was not given to men once and for all to make the distinction in this world. What happened in the depths of the soul when divine grace came upon one was a secret. In spite of his profound probings of the soul's operation, he admitted that no human being had access to that secret place. "Our wisdom and discerning, with respect to the hearts of men, is not much to be trusted. We can see but a little way into the nature of the soul, and the depths of man's heart."[136]

Clearly Edwards's new sense was important, but it did not limit the understanding of divine things if he meant his typology to be understood by all conditions of mankind. Its principal value was to distinguish between what men commonly could be expected to know of religious matters and the grasping of the existential and participative significance of these truths for one's personal life. Typology was one way of inspiring in people that existential knowledge about God and the drama of salvation. But for that appropriation only God and the self were responsible, and when it happened Edwards described it as a new regenerate sense.

What had his typology done to nature, we ask again. On the one hand, he exalted it by making of it a treasure-house of images and types that bespoke spiritual truths of a high order. In another sense he debased it by making it a handmaid of the superior world until the last vestiges of its immediate impact on the senses were lost. It was beautiful but marred. It was God's work, but only of a lower order when compared to the spiritual world. And at last it would pass away, as would all transitory earthly beauties. The Valley's beauties and order stand condemned, having done their work in inspiring images and types that far excelled anything that they possessed in their own right. Symbolism had the last word.

5

Nature, Morality, and Holiness

AMONG the learned of the eighteenth century, few words carried more authority and prestige than *nature*. In no small part the enthusiasm with which the word was embraced was due to its ambiguous meaning. In its most obvious sense the word signified the entire range of sensed physical objects that encircled human life. But science was pushing beyond so naive a meaning and in doing so increasingly laid bare the laws that gave order to the apparent diversity of the physical world. Nature was no longer what one saw and felt around oneself, but was the order itself. Nature not only "obeyed" laws, but essentially was order as dictated by laws. Once this identification of nature with laws and principles was made, it was not uncommon to suppose that these laws and principles described nature not only as it was but also as it ought to be. In this way nature as description was surreptitiously turned into a norm that proved adaptable to human affairs. In some fashion or other nature was seen as a standard by which to judge what was acceptable by rational people. To speak of an act, thought, or belief as being in accord with nature was to stake a claim for its undeniable truth, for it represented the essential correctness believed to exist in physical and law-abiding nature. By this indefinite standard social and political arrangements and morality generally could be estimated as to their relative validity. Nature had become a norm to which "right-thinking," rational people could repair, undisturbed by whatever opinions otherwise divided them. Here was a solid basis by which to guide human life. If one believed in God, then nature was His creation, which showed in all phases how human life was to be lived. If one did not believe in God, there still stood nature accomplishing the same end. Nature provided common ground for both believer and doubter. However, in fact, as the social and political events of the century showed, the word *nature* settled few important disputes. *Nature* could be bent to the interests of its proponents. When used conservatively it sanctioned any already settled social and political order on the assumption that this order reflected the steady, unchanging, and universal condition of physical nature. In the service of a more radical outlook, *nature* stood for human rights that were suppressed by the status quo defended by the conservatives. Both parties appealed to nature as a norm of what was right, but each party read nature according to its own interests. In religious matters the same clash of interests existed. Free-thinkers latched on to *nature*, with its correlate of right reason, to deny the legitimacy of religion—that is, Christianity, with its appeal to the supernatural and miracles. Less radical thinkers salvaged what they could by championing belief in a God of nature shorn of most of the attributes of the biblical deity. Edwards, like many others who held to more traditional religious beliefs, was called upon to interpret nature and reason in such a way that their importance would not be endangered by the supernaturalism of the Christian faith. He had to do justice to nature and yet give an account of spiritual realities that did not reduce them to a nature conceived in merely physical terms. However, nature as a system of laws and principles from the mind of God was acceptable to him. In that respect Edwards was quite in tune with a major segment of learned opinion of his period. The difference from that opinion was to show itself in how he employed these laws and principles in respect to the religious and moral life.

Edwards accepted nature as meaning the actuality of the sensible corporeal and external world. This usage is especially evident in his youthful "Diary," where no doubt was expressed as to the physical reality of his body in conflict with his appetites and religious ponderings. His correspondence with friends abroad and with the Princeton trustees shows the same unsophisticated acceptance of physical nature. Even his typology that referred to the actuality of historical events and natural objects in the Bible was based upon what he believed were concrete realities. The symbolism in the "Personal Narrative" followed the same pattern. In some periods of his life nature was physically real to him. However, his interest in science, the metaphysics of idealism, and his sense of the spiritual world pointed him in a different direction. Beyond this external and physically sensed world was another one. He repeatedly stated that this sensible world was but a shadow of the spiritual, and this was a large step in the direction of recognizing nature as consisting in a system of laws and principles akin to spiritual reality. In his most extreme statements he totally denied the existence of physical matter, bodies, as he said, having "no proper being of their own." That he had problems with consistently working out this view of nature as idea I have already demonstrated, but it was the most compelling of his conceptions of nature. In nature as sensibly experienced he found the principles of its orderliness, and upon them much of the order of the spiritual and ideal world depended. Nature was the ideas themselves, the "naked ideas" he once had sought, manifested in external nature but not confined to that domain. The word *nature* stood for a harmonious system of ideas existing by virtue of human perception and God's knowledge. Therefore to speak of nature was to all intents and purposes to speak of a metaphysic of nature rather than of a visible, tangible and existing world independent of human consciousness. This metaphysic of nature I suggest was the "nature" that exercised a profound and determinative influence on Edwards's view of the religious and ethical life.

This contention does not at a stroke eliminate for Edwards the importance of sensibly perceived nature. Analogy drawn from the ordinary world of human affairs or nature was still appealed to for understanding spiritual matters. Edwards, for example, used what transpired in daily experience to clarify what went on in the higher world when he wrote, "We never could have any notion what understanding or volition, love or hatred are, either in created spirits or in God, if we never experienced what understanding and volition, love and hatred are in our own minds."[1] The superior or real world might itself be ideal, but there still remained that inferior world from which truth could be drawn. This opinion was widely shared by other thinkers of the period. George Turnbull contended that natural philosophy, when carried through to the end, reduced phenomena to "good general laws" that became moral philosophy. Bishop Thomas Burnet went farther, to claim that since moral and natural phenomena were both part of God's world, "they run the same course and are so proportional to each other that man's moral and spiritual states may be gauged by examining the condition of nature." It is not clear what meaning of nature he had in mind, but the connection between two different kinds of experience is evident. Berkeley himself is credited with having compared gravity to benevolence and social attraction on the grounds that throughout "the moral and intellectual as well as the natural and corporeal" worlds there was "a certain correspondence of parts, similitude of operation and unity of design."[2] Edwards might have agreed in varying degrees with each of these comments as analogies, but Turnbull seems to have come the closest to Edwards's intent in respect to moral thought. When nature is reduced to its principles and laws, it did for Edwards convert into moral philosophy, as Turnbull suggested. And to describe nature metaphysically was to describe ideal reality itself, and at the same time to lay a foundation for analogy.

For Edwards God's world was not only an analogical or typological one, but a coherent reality where laws and principles discernible in external nature also operated in the realm of spirit. From the beginning he had been aware of the order, harmony, and beauty of the nature about him. But for his questing mind it was not sufficient to behold and revel in this beauty. He sought the root ideas by which this beauty was made possible. And he found them in the forms of attraction, cohesion, consent, proportionality, and symmetry.[3] But these principles, when expressed in the metaphysics of nature, were not to be understood simply as analogies, but as the very structure of a reality that encompassed both sensible and ideal reality. The entire world, being one under God, could be expected to exhibit in both areas the same overriding principles by which beauty or excellence was created. Accordingly, the reason why the "sweet harmony between the various parts of the universe" was "an image of mutual love" was that the same structures were operative at both levels, the world being one.[4] Edwards spelled out this insight in Miscellany 651, in which he argued that inanimate, animate, and human beings were all governed by "exactly the same laws." This he took to be a strong argument that the world had but one Creator and governor. The analogy "between the corporeal and spiritual parts of the creation" further established his thesis that the whole is the creation of but one wisdom and design.[5] In short, the analogies Edwards found throughout nature that pointed to and expressed spiritual reality hinged upon the prior assumption of the unity of the whole world whose laws and principles operated at every level. Analogy without this grounding in the unity and relationship of all things would have been left without a metaphysical reason. It is not difficult, therefore, to see his treatment of true virtue as exhibiting the manner in which morality also was in conformity with the ideal structures underlying the analogies found in nature. The metaphysics of nature enabled him to give an account of virtue that partook of the beauty of the corporeal world, since both manifested the same principles of order.

In the first instance true virtue for Edwards was "that consent, propensity and union of heart to being in general, which is immediately exercised in a general good will." The beauty of this disposition rested not on discord or discontent, but as any intelligent being is in some way always related to being in general, it consisted in "union and consent with the great whole."[6] Clearly then, consent or agreement was at the heart of true virtue. However, an interesting question may be raised as to the status of consent in the wider context of Edwards's thought. Was consent an actual feature of nature sensibly experienced or otherwise interpreted? Or was it a unique relation between spiritual beings, quite independent of sensible nature? In favor of the latter option stands Edwards's explicit admission that his use of the word *consent* in reference to the excellence of bodies was one borrowed from spiritual beings. Consent, so considered, made of the consents of corporeal nature an analogy to the higher world. Furthermore it underlined the unique status of what Edwards called "proper consent." "There is no proper consent but that of minds," he wrote, "which when it is of minds towards minds, it is love and when of minds towards other things it is choice."[7] Yet the word *consent* was peculiarly appropriate in respect to nature in the light of other aspects of Edwards's philosophy and science. When we bear in mind his conviction that the whole world was one under God, we can understand that, however the realm of nature be characterized, it possessed features that had their counterparts in the superior world of spirit, as did the superior world in the lower one. His essay on the "Reality of the World" was replete with references to the "many sorts of consent" in the corporeal world, wherein lay "the sweetest and most charming beauty."[8] He intended those consents to be images of the beauty of the spiritual world, but it is significant that the best way he had of delineating this beauty was to turn first to the consents in the corporeal world. There he found the evidence of a consent that not only reflected but also gave form to spiritual consent.

The notion of consent or agreement may be seen in a larger perspective when nature is considered metaphysically. Excellence in respect to bodies, Edwards had made clear, depended on similarity between them, or agreement. If there was disagreement, the result produced pain or lack of pleasure in perceiving beings. This state he labeled "the greatest and only evil," whereas agreement was "the greatest and only good." Excellence or beauty then depended on consents or agreements, the lack of which gave rise to deformity or "false beauty."[9] This insight allowed Edwards to conclude that "the beauty of figures and motion, when one part has such consonant proportion with the rest as representing a general agreeing and consenting together" is "very much the image of love in all parts of a society united by a sweet consent and charity of heart." In a slightly different sense he suggested "sensible things, by virtue of the harmony and proportion that is seen in them, carry the appearance of perceiving and willing being."[10] In these passages analogy was used, but they also cast consent or agreement in terms of metaphysical reality. It is not purely sensibly experienced nature that is at stake, but certain metaphysical principles such as harmony and proportion that govern consent. Nature is here being interpreted in conformity with metaphysical principles that are detectable in nature as sensibly experienced, but are extracted to be in conformity with Edwards's contention that nature was essentially idea, and for him reality was mentalistic. Consent then, as idea, was embedded in the very nature of reality, and had a wider meaning than that attributed to consent as a spiritual relation between human beings. Consent could then be construed not only as an analogy between nature as sensibly experienced and the spiritual dimension, but as part and parcel of reality. I take it that in part this was Fiering's meaning in denying that the relation between the physical world and God's continuous activity was simply a matter of analogy. "There is an actual metaphysical connection," he wrote, "between the perceived world and divine activity, explicable in terms of Edwards's philosophical idealism."[11]

Edwards's scientific speculation on the universe also gave support to the more inclusive meaning of consent. He had paid especial attention to the power of attraction, cohesion, and gravity in nature. Without gravity the whole corporeal world would vanish, and atoms cleave to each other by this same power of attraction, which insures cohesion. "There must," Edwards concluded, "be an universal attraction in the whole system of things from the beginning to the end." Indeed, so powerful and pervasive was the power of attraction that if there was the least change in one atom, all other atoms would also be changed, thus making the universe other than what it now is.[12] Similarly changes in the least particles of the human body, Edwards surmised, would cause a thought to arise, "which in length of time (yea, and that not very great) might occasion a vast alteration through the whole world of mankind."[13] Thus the mutual attraction operative in nature can be seen as testimony to the idea of consent, for as things are drawn to each other and affect each other, they do so by means of what is similar in each part to the other. In seizing upon the power of attraction in nature, Edwards had grasped a fundamental metaphysical principle, whose influence was not confined to natural phenomena. Attraction was but a form of consent which, understood as metaphysical truth, was writ large over all of God's creation. The consent of minds was the supreme instance of an all-embracing metaphysic whose agreements unified the whole universe. Therefore it was not an exception to the way the universe acted, but its chief exemplification at the conscious level. To this fact Edwards paid tribute by defining excellency as consent of being to being and supremely in "being's consent to entity," that is, God. On the basis of this consent he could go on to add that "the more consent is, and the more extensive, the greater is the excellency."[14]

At the human level consent is an affection. When experienced consciously, attraction or consent as an aspect of the metaphysics of nature becomes vastly more than an abstract unitive relation of inert particles. It is a deeply felt union of selves with selves or selves with God. It is love. But love or affection was to be no unbridled passion. At the height of the Great Awakening Edwards had come to understand that intense surges of emotion taken as evidence of grace needed to be in subservience to principle, and for that principle his metaphysic of nature came into play in another way.

This principle was proportionality. He had developed the importance of this concept in his account of beauty in the corporeal world where delicate ratios and proportion reigned. When he spoke of excellency, he turned to descriptions of equalities, ratios, and proportions exhibited by globes, circles, and parallel and perpendicular lines. Everywhere he looked, Edwards found excellency to inhere in "harmony, symmetry and proportion." "There is no other way that sensible things can consent one to another but by equality, or by likeness, or by proportion." Harmony was observable about him in notes of music, the beauty of figures and motion, the pen drawings of flowers, the human body, the features of a face or the structure of buildings, all of which were examples of proportional consent. "I can conceive of no other reason why equality and proportion should be pleasing to him that perceives, but only that it has an appearance of consent."[15] Proportionality and consent were fellow principles in the idea of excellency and beauty.

Nowhere was this connection between consent and proportionality more evident to Edwards than in his conception of God, who by any definition of perfection manifested true virtue at its highest point. Proportion was then not simply to be confined to things in the corporeal world. Like consent, it was to be understood as ingrained in the ideal reality of the world. Although Edwards plainly stated that there was no proportion between universal being, that is, God, and finite being, no matter how great the degree of the latter, this did not signify that God's love of Himself failed in respect to proportionality.[16] God's "infinite beauty" lay in "his mutual love of himself" and this was to be seen in the doctrine of the Trinity.[17] Since God was supremely excellent and since any single entity by itself would lack duality and therefore the basis for consent between itself and other entities, there must be a plurality in God by which He exercises a "mutual love of himself."[18] This is a rendering of true virtue in God that employs another metaphysical principle, that of duality or polarity, without which consent would be impossible. Duality also plays its part when God's knowledge of Himself as the proper object of love or consent is considered. To know Himself, something "distinct from his meer direct existence" must be known, just as in human beings there must be something that occasions reflection that is differentiated from the reflection itself. Since God is supremely excellent, He must as it were have Himself as the object of reflection, and this is made possible by the presence of Himself in the Trinity.[19] And what He knows is that He is the greatest being and therefore, by the principle of proportionality, rightly loves or consents to Himself. Above all else, since "that object who has the most of being, or has the greatest share of existence, 'other things being equal' . . . will have the greatest share of the propensity and benevolent affections of the heart."[20] This being so in respect to persons, so also it is true for God, whose being far exceeds that of all else.

In *The End For Which God Created the World* Edwards rehearsed the theme of proportionality and quantity of being by setting up a hypothetical situation to make his point. He postulated that some imaginary eternal being of disinterested perfect wisdom and rectitude could judge the proper balance of regard due to God on the one hand, and the created order on the other. This being, having weighed the degrees of existence and moral excellence in both, would of course find that God outweighed the remainder of the world "in such proportion" that He should have the "greatest share of regard." However, in fact, there was no need for this hypothetical third party, since God Himself possessed the perfect discernment and rectitude by which He impartially judged in His own favor.[21] Thus, by the principle of proportionality God was established as the sole object of true virtue, for both Himself and human beings.

Edwards proposed that even in heaven proportionality reigned in respect to true virtue. There the "symmetry and proportion in God's workmanship" found in the world functioned in the celestial love enjoyed by the saints. In heaven the saints would practice affections in perfect degree and proportion. "Love is in proportion to the perfection and amiableness of the objects beloved, and therefore it must necessarily cause delight in them when they see that the happiness and glory of others are in proportion to their amiableness, and so in proportion to their love to them." Or more simply stated, "Just in proportion as any person is beloved, in the same proportion is his love desired and prized."[22] If anywhere true virtue would be realized to its fullest, heaven would indeed be the place.

As proportion ruled the display of true virtue in heaven, so it also did on earth. As it played its part in the production of harmonious sound and color vibrations, so it also applied to spiritual harmonies, where "the proportions are vastly oftener redoubled and respect more beings." In fact, to get to the root of the matter Edwards claimed that being was itself "nothing else but proportion."[23] No wonder then that true virtue, which had to do with consent to being, should itself reflect proportionality. Its validity was to be in proportion to the greatness of the object to which it was addressed, the infinite Being or Being in general. And its expression among fellow human beings was to follow the same pattern. When writing in justification of revivalism Edwards had let it be known that Christian love should be extended "to one and another only in that proportion in which the image of God is seen in them."[24] And by the time he penned *The Nature of True Virtue* he had not deviated from the conviction that true virtue as love should be meted out to others in agreement with proportionality. In this would also be a beauty. The amiableness of true virtue lay in consent and benevolence and "in a proportion compounded of the greatness of the benevolent being, in the degree of being and the degree of benevolence." It followed then that one who loves Being in general will value the same good will wherever he sees it and will value it even more if he sees it in two beings rather than in one. Then there would be more being favoring being on a strictly quantitative basis. What this means is that when true virtue does its work, it fastens on other human beings who have the same temper of benevolence and consent to being in general. One loves others in proportion to the degree of being and benevolence they have. "And that is to love beings in proportion to their dignity."[25]

But Edwards's enchantment with the idea of proportionality in this case comes to a strange end, for it stands at complete odds with the Christian message of salvation. That message one might have thought extended true virtue or love to those who most needed it, not only to those who already possessed it. If love to others was to be meted out on the basis of their amount of being and benevolence, Christian virtue could not only lack spontaneity but be limited to a very small segment of the human population. Edwards might well have settled for a "small segment" with his idea of election of the saints. But would this not be a far remove from Jesus' words criticizing those who love only those who love them? (cf. Matt. 5:47) It is precisely those who lack consent to being and lack moral excellence that most need the ministrations of true Christian love. Or, as Paul Tillich read the Christian Gospel, it had to do with "the acceptance of the unacceptable." Edwards, on the other hand, was so far under the spell of proportionality that he accepted the commonplace truth that like attracted like in due proportion on earth as in heaven.[26]

In his earlier writings Edwards had addressed this flaw in his later metaphysical calculations. There he pictured true virtue, although slightly tainted by ulterior motives, as being directed to both the good and the bad. "We should do good to all men as we have opportunity" that they may be benefited and won to Christ. The truly virtuous person is obliged to do good to enemies, for that is "the only retaliation that becomes us as Christians. . . ." True love is universal benevolence and good will, and properly embraces friends and enemies, the thankful and unthankful.[27] The *True Virtue* glancingly struck the same theme when, in distinguishing secondary virtue from true virtue, he stressed that the general beauty of true virtue was comprehensive "as related to everything with which it stands connected."[28] From that assertion it would follow that since all people are related to Being in general in one way or another, benevolence should be exercised to all persons regardless of their spiritual estate.

When all is told of true virtue, it remains a correct relation to Being in general, consisting of cordial consent or love to Being in general, exercised in proportion both as to the greatness of the deity and as to one's fellow men in proportion to their dignity or degree of being and excellence. The priority of being, however, seems to have been the foundation of the beauty and excellence found in true virtue. Had he not stated that "existence or entity is that into which all excellency is to be resolved"? The greatness of being, that is, God, "considered alone is the more excellent because he partakes more of being. . . ."[29] Accordingly, nothing could be of the nature of true virtue unless it had for its direct and immediate object "being in general or the great system of universal existence."[30] What was not clear was why people should be incited to love and practice benevolence to others by a vivid awareness of Being in general. Why should greatness of being in infinite degree evoke cordial consent to itself or in turn prompt love to created beings? At most sheer "is-ness" in infinite degree that exceeded all finitude might produce wonder, awe, or fear, but certainly not cordial consent. That may be the reason Edwards could say "No proportion is the cause or ground of the existence of such a thing as benevolence to being," although elsewhere he had already affirmed that being was nothing else but proportion. A shift in his thought seems to have occurred at this juncture when he asserted that proportion of being "is the consequence of the existence of benevolence and not the ground of it."[31]

This pronouncement looks like a reversal of his emphasis upon the priority of being in true virtue, but it was an insight quite in keeping with his claim that God's goodness "moved him to give both being and beauty" to objects in the world.[32] Edwards supported this priority of benevolence in God by an example drawn from nature. Bodies that attract each other do so in proportion to their degree of matter, but—and this was his point—this proportion is due to the mutual attraction itself, not simply to proportionality. Thus, in respect to being's consent to being, he could write, "If being, in itself considered, were not pleasing, being's consent to being would not be pleasing, nor would disagreeing with being be displeasing." Consent then, as one central feature of true virtue or excellency, was inherent in being itself. God as "the infinite, universal and all-comprehending existence" had within Himself not simply a preponderance of sheer existence, but His being by its very nature was excellent and beautiful, and this was what attracted human beings to loving consent. One could love Being in general because God as Being in general exhibited loving consent in his very nature. Existence, of which God was the supreme exemplar, was "that into which all excellency is to be resolved."[33] There could be no distinction between being and excellence. The two were inextricably bound together.

This alliance of being with excellence escaped the notice of some of his early critics, who seized upon his frequent references to being as such to show the inadequacy of his conception of true virtue. *Being* is one of those essential metaphysical terms that either gathers to itself all the sensed differentiation of actual existence or is one so vague as to be devoid of any specific meaning. In the first sense the term *being* adds nothing to the fact that things, people, laws, and so on, exist. In the second sense the term can be bent to the design of the one who uses it. Although Edwards did not in the final analysis intend either of these meanings, his manner of writing gave ample opportunity for critics to blast him for playing fast and loose with an idea void of identifying attributes. The Reverend William Hart so read Edwards on true virtue, and concluded that Edwards's notion of Being in general was offered to religious folk as a being without perception, will, or ethical qualities. Being, abstractly considered, Hart argued, "is neither wise nor foolish, neither morally good nor evil, neither self-existent nor created and dependent upon neither God nor creature." Most cuttingly in the face of Edwards's talk of benevolence, he added, "It has no relation to the benevolent mind." In short, being dressed up as Being in general in infinite degree was a featureless metaphysical abstraction and not at all the God of Christian faith.[34] Whatever the shortcomings of Hart's little book, and there were many, he succeeded in fastening on Edwards the charge that abstract metaphysical reasoning produced something that did not in the least resemble the God of the Bible and vital piety. One could not identify the conclusions of abstract speculation with a deity that loved, decided, hated, judged, and redeemed humanity. Being in general was a shapeless something or other that just was and did nothing. Edwards's love of metaphysics had run him aground on the hard rock of the difference between his Calvinist biblical faith and metaphysics. Hart seems to have taken the alternative that being was an empty notion. Robert Hall, an English clergyman, took the opposite view, namely that being in general referred to every single item in the universe. The inadequacy of Edwards's notion of morality lay in what Hall took to be the necessity of a truly virtuous person cordially to consent to every single item or person in the world. And that was an impossible goal. Instead of beginning with an affection for something called Being in general, Hall argued, men should first be made benevolent and unselfish in their private affections. "As in the operations of intellect we proceed from the contemplation of individuals to the formation of general abstractions, so in the development of the passions, in like manner we advance from private to public affections." Otherwise men are taught "to love the whole species more by loving every particular part less." Furthermore, in agreement with Hart, the notion of pursuing the good of the whole in its abstractness "is a motive so loose and indeterminate, and embraces such an infinity of relations, that before we could be certain what action it prescribed, the season of action would be past."[35] For Hall it was not sin that prevented men from cordially consenting to Being in general. It was sheer entanglement in metaphysical relations that frustrated any efforts in that direction. Even divine grace or "a new sense" would seem to have been incapable of untangling the formidable network of relations into which Edwards had snared people.

There is a specious validity in Hall's analysis, for which Edwards himself was partly to blame. Edwards had written that "among created beings one single person must be looked upon as inconsiderable in comparison of the generality; and so his interest is of little importance compared with the interest of the whole system." In fact when the interest of a single person or part of the whole is held to be of more importance than the whole of being, it is vicious and sinful.[36] Furthermore Edwards's insistence upon proportionality and the quantification of being as essential to true virtue opened him to the criticism of Hall. His famous, if not notorious note on love "in proportion to the degree of existence" led to his claim that "an archangel must be supposed to have more existence and to be every way farther removed from nonentity, than a worm."[37] This observation undoubtedly owed much to Edwards's hierarchical view of nature in a Neoplatonic mode of thought. In his *End for Which God Created the World* he had described God's beauty, power, and wisdom as poured forth as from a fountain, or the sun, thus making created beings the lower in the order the less they participated in God's nature. Saints, however, received the outpouring of God's nature and thus resonated back to God his original emanation, and stood higher.[38] If Hall had read this work, he would have found further evidence that the theory of the quantity of being and excellence gave shape to an ethical and metaphysical outlook that moved in the opposite direction from his insistence upon the importance of individuals and the danger of their loving Being in general more and "loving each other less."

But had these critics read Edwards correctly as to the meaning of Being in general? Did Edwards mean to equate Being in general with every single feature of the created world? Or did he mean that Being in general was a term without specifiable meaning, as Hart supposed? The first alternative was a truism that yielded no religious or metaphysical rewards. And the second was in danger of becoming identified with nothing in particular. And as Edwards had announced that "there should absolutely be nothing at all is utterly impossible . . . ," a state of absolute nothing is a state of absolute contradiction.[39] Even to talk about nothing except in relation to something that exists is to suppose being in some sense. Thus ontology asserts itself in the very texture of rational discourse. Being therefore could not be a void of which everything and nothing could be said with equal validity. It had structure, and at a minimum it was proportion, which was one sign of its excellency or beauty. Excellence would be impossible if being were not presupposed as its ontological ground, and being without proportion would not be excellent or beautiful. And to Edwards's mind Being in general was that supreme excellence. The dividing point between Edwards and his critics was his firm, but often untidily expressed conviction that Being in general was not any kind of being or sum of beings that existed in the finite world, with God regarded merely as a superior form thereof, but essentially of the same kind.[40]

At this point it is important to recall again that for Edwards being itself was nothing else but proportion. This enigmatic statement presupposed a plurality of relations within being, in respect to which proportionality had definite meaning. "One alone, without reference to any more, cannot be excellent," since without relations there would be no place for consent, the archetype of which was the Trinity itself.[41] God as Being in general was the unique model of true excellence, whose internal relations were adumbrated in relations with nature and perceiving beings. Being in general was not then to be regarded as a structureless "something" without attributes, subject to deformation by human desires or ignorance. God was not a simple unity, but a complex one constituted of an infinite number of relations, the principal one of which was consent. In this lay His goodness, beauty, and excellence, which acted as a lure for saintly souls. Being in general was obviously related to being in the world, but as the power and excellence that permeated and upheld them. Yet it was not totally identified with them. The world was *one* under God, but it *was* not God or Being in general. The difference Edwards had made clear when he stated that there was no proportion between the greatness of the natural, finite world and God.[42] So God was in and with the world, but never to be assimilated to it. This was not pantheism in any literal sense, as I have previously argued, but a metaphysical position that is best described as panentheism, which retains the transcendence of God to His world and saves divine engagement with it at all points. In that lay His sovereignty.

One who lived or consented to Being in general was not, as Hall supposed, driven first to establish benevolent relations with every single human before ascending to a love of Being in general. Nor, for Edwards, was this a state in which motivation would be loose and indeterminate. In loving Being in general in proportion to its being and excellence, one is also disposed to dispense love to other human beings in proportion to their degrees of existence and benevolence. Contrary to Hall's opinion, Edwards saw that private affections left to themselves or energized by the most strenuous human effort never overcome their self-interested position. They do not of themselves expand to encompass all beings or Being in general. And even if ever larger numbers of finite beings are encompassed with affection, one does not finally bridge the gap between natural affections and love of God for His own sake and not for what one hopes to get from such a relation. To consent to Being in general is first to chasten, purify, and convert private affections at their root and open them to the widest possible comprehension of reality. Then they reflect the beauty, goodness, wisdom, and power resident in Being in general and radiate the same to other beings. And this state of affairs transcends mere morality. It is holiness, the supreme goal of the spiritual life.

Most people do not live on the breathless heights of true virtue or holiness. The moral habitat of natural man is a secondary kind of morality that has its own kind of beauty, but one that does not reach to the level of spiritual enjoyment. To this kind of morality Edwards paid a great deal of attention in order to set off its inadequacy from the standpoint of true virtue.

Edwards's treatment of natural morality begins with his announcement that the consent found in spiritual beauty has its counterpart in the beauty of natural things, even in inanimate things. It consists, as we might expect, in regularity, order, uniformity, symmetry, proportion, and harmony.[43] As such, it is some image of true spiritual beauty. The correspondence also includes consent, but at this point the first difference between it and true virtue appears. Both types of morality involve consent, but true virtue is set off from natural morality by its cordial consent. Natural agreement, although it is an image of genuine union, is entirely different, "the will, disposition or affection of the heart having no concern in it, but consisting only in uniformity and consent of nature, form, quantity etc." Cordial consent, on the other hand, "consists in concord and union of mind and heart." The first kind of consent is due to natural causes or principles; the second is an insight into the union itself. It is the immediate view of that wherein the beauty fundamentally lies and is therefore pleasing to the virtuous mind.[44] Secondary beauty is a term that applies not only to material and external things, but also to immaterial realities. "If uniformity and proportion be the things that affect and appear agreeable to the sense of beauty, then," asked Edwards, "why should not uniformity and proportion affect the same sense in immaterial things as well . . . if there be equal capacity of discerning it in both?[45] His emphasis on the principle of proportionality first seen in nature has led one author to argue that proportionality is the essential factor in secondary virtue and has no application to true virtue.[46] Yet, as demonstrated, proportionality had its part to play in several ways in respect to true virtue and the nature of God, the perfect being. Consequently, proportionality cannot be used as the identifying mark of secondary virtue, important as it was.

This fact becomes equally apparent in opposition to this same author's criticism that beauty was for Edwards the clue to his thought, for beauty, even of the purely spiritual kind, was marked by proportionality. To speak meaningfully of Edwards's notion of beauty demanded that it include not only affection or consent, but right knowledge and structure. The beauty of true virtue depended upon cordial consent, but equally important was the cognitive factor. Consent, no matter how cordial, would be left without direction as to its proper object and range without knowledge of God. Edwards was keenly aware in the revivals of the danger that people of heated emotions would seize upon any uprush of feelings as indicative of divine grace. To guard against this antinomian threat he maintained that correct knowledge was necessary. Although he admitted "it is not easy, precisely to fix the limits of man's capacity as to love of God; yet in general we may determine that his capacity of love is coextended with his capacity of knowledge. The exercise of the understanding opens the way for the other faculty," that is, affection.[47] He had previously made his point clear by stating that the first objective ground of gracious affections was "the transcendently excellent and amiable nature of divine things as they are in themselves; and not any conceived relation they bear to self, or self-interest."[48] And in the *True Virtue* he reemphasized the point by claiming that "the first object of a virtuous benevolence," simply considered, was Being in general.[49] Unfortunately for man, sin had entered to mar and disfigure this beautiful relationship, and love of God had been misdirected to self and accordingly reduced its range to finite entities. "Sin, like some powerful astringent, contracted his soul to the very small dimensions of selfishness."[50] Breadth and comprehensiveness of knowledge had been surrendered, and as a result affections, without that necessary knowledge, had been devoted to a "private circle or system of beings" that were but a fraction of the whole of existence, inclusive of God. In the case of true virtue, knowledge was enlarged and invigorated by divine grace, and centered then on God alone.[51] And in that was beauty.

Equally important to beauty of true and secondary virtue was the need of structure, which proportionality provided. The beauty Edwards attributed to true virtue could not be realized without harmony among beings, which presupposed not only consent but proportionality. As nature was a harmonious system, so also, thought Edwards, was true virtue. In his analysis of excellence he had concluded that proportion was more pleasing than deformity or disproportion because "disproportion or inconsistency is contrary to being," which is nothing else but proportion.[52] So being, Being in general, and the affections directed to Being in general must in high degree be beautiful because of the proportionality that insured structure.[53]

Without these three factors of cordial consent, knowledge, and proportionality, beauty could not exist as a feature of true virtue. But no one of them by itself could distinguish secondary or inferior beauty from true beauty. However, if one chooses to concentrate on the end product of these three factors, it may be said that beauty was the central idea of his system, but it must not be forgotten that that beauty depended on the integral relations between cordial consent, knowledge, and proportionality that made beauty possible. When these relations are placed to the forefront, then one can agree with Fiering that beauty "is not itself an ultimate category." It is a derivative of relations.[54]

What then sets off secondary beauty or common morality from true virtue? Proportionality by itself cannot do it. Cordial consent fails the test, since intensity of the emotions can be found among even the greatest of sinners, whose affections rest upon finite entities including themselves. Knowledge does not of itself draw the line between

secondary and true virtue. Yet there must be a line to be drawn
between the two.

The primary place where the distinction occurs is in a consideration of what is meant by cordial consent. In one important sense it is
a warm-hearted agreement between the soul and Being in general. It
is a matter of the affections in their most dynamic operations. It is an
immediate sensation or intuition, not one built upon arguments, "any
more than tasting the sweetness of honey, or perceiving the harmony
of a tune, is by argumentation or connections and consequences."[55]
There is something more than argument in cordial consent. That
factor is intuitive insight or knowledge. What makes true virtue
appealing is not simply the intensity of one's affections, but the
perception of the union itself, and that quality secondary virtue or
beauty lacks.[56] This higher kind of knowledge was for Edwards quite
different from the natural appreciation of agreement and proportion
that men find in both nature and moral matters.

Secondary virtue is due to a law of nature that God has implanted
in all rational persons, but they "do not reflect in that particular
agreement and proportion which . . . is the ground and rule of beauty
in the case." They remain ignorant of what in fact constitutes the
beauty of the world, but are pleased with it nevertheless. They are
unable to penetrate to the essence of beauty, as does true virtue when
it stirs the heart to cordial consent. As such, secondary virtue is an
entirely different thing from a truly virtuous taste and "has no connection with virtue."[57]

Cordial consent as a form of cognition sees what indeed makes
beauty to be itself, and that is to see the proper relation between the
affections and their true object. Natural, unconverted people could,
with an intensity equal to that assumed to exist in true virtue, relish
and enjoy relations among things in the natural world and even
justice in ethical matters. Their affections, however, were thereby
fixed upon finite objects, including themselves. True virtue or valid
gracious affections fixed upon that which possessed the highest degree of excellence and being. As he had written in the "Miscellanies,"
"Tis from the nature of the object loved rather than from the degree of
the principle [love] in the lover."[58] Therefore secondary virtue is set
off from true virtue not by the degree of affection or agreement
exercised, but by the object to which that agreement yields itself, and
that is God, the perfect being. This insight led Edwards to diverge
from other benevolence and moral-sense philosophers who to his
mind had confused secondary with primary moral beauty. Of them,
with Hutcheson and Wollaston particularly in mind, he commented,
"They do not wholly exclude a regard to the Deity but yet mention it

so slightly, that they leave one room and reason to suspect they
esteem it as less important and a subordinate part of true morality."
But if God plays some part in morality, he added, then it must be that
respect to God is the chief ingredient in true virtue.[59] Philosophies
that teach benevolence or generosity toward mankind and other
virtues without "apprehension of God's supreme glory and worthi-
ness and an answerable supreme esteem of and love to Him" are "not
true schemes of philosophy" and are "fundamentally wrong."[60] There
may indeed be a moral sense in human beings that enables them to be
gratified by displays of virtue, and prompts them to love others who
love them, but this moral sense is at a secondary level of the ethical
manifold and "is entirely different from a sense or relish of the
original essential beauty of true virtue."[61] The fault remains in the
moral-sense theory when its proponents wrongly suppose that this
natural virtue is identical with true virtue. Yet the natural moral
sense "so far as it is disinterested" is the same as conscience, which of
course was part of man's natural moral equipment.[62] Nevertheless,
the omission of the divine object by definition condemns this philosophy as totally inadequate.

This inadequacy bears as its consequence the lack of comprehensive insight and affection. Whereas true virtue directs benevolence to
Being in general, the natural moral sense is always limited to "private
systems" and that term refers not only to self-interested individuals
but to the most far-reaching, inclusive systems of finite beings. Humanity for Edwards would still be a "private system," because all
existence is not exhausted by any collection of human, living, or
inanimate entities for that matter. As long as natural affection embraces only a part of universal existence, it "bears no proportion to
the great all-comprehending system."[63] Thus to rest one's affections
on that which is disproportionate to Being in general is to settle for
an inferior type of virtue, which when regarded as selfishness is in
outright opposition to true virtue.

Self-interest then suffers from a myopic view of existence. "The
reason why men are so ready to take their private affections for true
virtue, is the narrowness of their views," and of course that means
they leave "the divine Being out of view" or regard him as "a kind of
shadowy, imaginary being."[64] Yet self-interest has its uses. It is necessary to society and by means of it men do disapprove of vices and
immorality and approve such virtues as meekness, peaceableness,
benevolence, charity, generosity, justice, and the social virtues in
general, which tend to the welfare of mankind.[65] Surely sinners seek
and love their own happiness, which is to be found in the esteem and
love others have for them, although again this yearning for happiness

is centered in self rather than graced by the disinterestedness that accompanies true benevolence. In an absolute sense Edwards was willing to affirm that the degree of men's happiness may be the same in saint and sinner when directed toward others, but he was quick to add, "the proportion that their love of self bears to their love for others, may not be the same."[66] Yet he was unwilling to deny that this kind of affection should be entirely abolished. It was needful for the good of man and society, and totally to root it out would be "to reproach and oppose the wisdom of the Creator."[67]

On the other hand he was loath to accept at face value the notion that self-love, following "the laws of nature," created mutual love. There was no metaphysical necessity for this to be the case, since to suppose that it could be otherwise implied no contradiction. To illustrate his point he plunged into a tangled argument that depended upon the operations of nature. Because bodies have solidity, cohesion, and gravitation toward the center of the earth, he argued, it did not follow by metaphysical necessity that "a weight suspended on the beam of a balance should have greater power to counterbalance a weight on the other side, when that body was at a distance from the fulcrum, than when it was near." There is no logical contradiction involved that it should be otherwise. Similarly there is no absolute metaphysical necessity, because there is an internal mutual attraction of the parts of the earth whereby the whole becomes one solid coherent body, that other bodies around it should also be attracted by it. The only contradiction that could occur would be due to the fact that these arrangements contradicted "that beautiful proportion and harmony, which the Author of Nature observes in the laws of nature." Edwards concluded by analogy, "By a like order of nature a man's love to those who love him, is no more than a certain expression or effect of self-love." Consequently, there is no more true virtue in a man's loving his friends from self-love than there is in the motive of self-love itself.[68]

This excursion into the natural realm may show that Edwards's thoughts on morality were never far distant from his metaphysics of nature, but it is doubtful that the arguments he proposed very much clarified the status of self-love. He certainly, for example, had not shown why "metaphysical necessity" and natural law were not both products of God's arbitrary will and therefore were indistinguishable from each other. He had instead virtually disavowed that there was any connection between "metaphysical necessity" and natural law, thus introducing confusion into his argument that presumably made self-love a natural law of human life.

Edwards seems to have been of two minds concerning the difference between this secondary virtue inclusive of self-love, moral sense, and conscience, and true virtue. He had made it clear that the two had nothing to do with each other, inferior virtue being in outright opposition to primary virtue. Yet there were strong connections between the two. Both were forms of beauty that inevitably conformed to the general definition of beauty as proportionality, agreement, and harmony. In fact, without recourse to ideas derived from secondary virtue Edwards would have been hard pressed to describe the higher beauty of true virtue. Instead he might well have been reduced to inarticulate ejaculations of delight over true virtue, as also he would have been over the taste of honey. Instead he wrote, "Some image of the true, spiritual, original beauty . . . consisting in being's consent to being, or the union of spiritual beings in a mutual propensity and affection of heart" was detectable in the beauty of sensed objects.[69] Although this opinion followed Edwards's tendency to believe that spiritual realities were models for inferior things, the converse was true, since in fact he had patterned his ethics upon what he had learned from his metaphysics of nature. The distinction between the two orders of morality also was endangered at another point, in spite of Edwards's claim that natural men had no access to true virtue. These same persons, he admitted, by natural conscience could approve true virtue "from that uniformity, equality, and justice which there is in it."[70] Apparently there was some limited access to true virtue by those who did not participate in it. They could at least recognize in it the principles derived from the metaphysics of nature.

Nevertheless, the gap between the two moralities was repeatedly emphasized. Edwards insisted that delight in natural beauty was in no way dependent on the possession of true virtue. Those elevated to the realm of true virtue did not therefore have a livelier appreciation of the beauty of "squares and cubes" or other indications of order in the world about them. Appreciation of the natural world was not increased in proportion to the height of one's virtue, as seen in the fact that "very vicious and lewd" persons possess a sense of natural beauty. So it must be obvious that as awareness of natural beauty is not dependent on appreciation of spiritual beauty, neither is appreciation of spiritual beauty dependent on that of natural beauty. Each is independent of the other.[71] Edwards had apparently changed his mind slightly on this point. In his *Religious Affections* he admitted that natural man might have a sense of the natural perfection of God, but he insisted that this sense more frequently occurred in the saints. By means of grace the saints' perception of the natural attributes of God was enhanced, and so also presumably would be the perception of those divine principles which constituted the beauty of the natural world. If this was the case, their delight in the natural world and the natural attributes of God that were seen in that world would be in proportion to the degree of one's true virtue represented in aesthetic sensitivity.[72] However, it did not follow that delight in natural beauty led automatically to delight in the spiritual beauty of true virtue. The relation between the two kinds of beauty was asymmetrical. Spiritual beauty would enhance sensitivity to natural beauty, but appreciation of natural beauty would never mount to the heights of spiritual beauty. There remained the dictum that there was no proportion between the whole of finite existence and the infinite Being, God. And on that ground Edwards was convinced, in spite of some evidence to the contrary, that no path led from natural morality to the beauty of true virtue. The intervening step of a "new sense" due to divine grace, which would span the gap, had to be taken.

There was another way of construing the nature of true virtue that was also largely influenced by Edwards's conception of nature. The world after all was one whole. It remained therefore to show how this idea of a unitary, harmonious world played its part in the structure of true virtue or holiness. This was accomplished by an insistence not only upon harmony of all parts of the sensed world, but preeminently by the notion of the hierarchy of all creation. This idea was what has come to be known as "The Great Chain of Being." Edwards, in keeping with this popular eighteenth-century notion, described the world of nature as one of a descending series of types of beings ranging from God downward through angels, men, animals, vegetation, and inanimate nature. The world as an object both of the senses and of spiritual perception was an organic harmony created or emanated from and presided over by the perfect being, God. If, as we have seen, Edwards's metaphysics of nature tended to analytically skeletonize both nature and virtue, the chain of being remedied that fault by spelling out an interdependent creation built on a vertical scale of being. Edwards was captivated by this essentially Neoplatonic scheme, which at one and the same time did justice to proportionality of beings and protected differences within the created world without breaching the difference between it and God. The chain-of-being concept extended into heaven as well as into the lower world. In heaven there would be some souls of a higher degree of being and excellence than those of lesser status. Above both stood the angels, with similar degrees of dignity, to whom the saints were subordinate. And below both those ranks were others filled by natural men, on down through animals with varying degrees of being until one reached inanimate nature, beyond which there would be nothing.

The social and political world found the same hierarchical principle at work. In his thoughts in "God's Moral Government" Edwards expressed his belief that God had so constituted all things with an eye to "beauty, good order and regulation, proportion and harmony" that the very system of the natural world in its seasons, in the formation of plants and the various parts of the human body, all reflected this divine order. Since mankind was the highest type of being within this world, possessed of intelligence, perception, mind, and action, it too shared in the pattern of subordination and superordination, lest by failing to obey the laws of social coherence humanity fall into discord, confusion, and ruin. As all natural bodies in the created world were united as individual entities [atoms?] in one body by mutual dependence and subserviency, so human society should also reflect the same order and harmony. Specifically, God has intended "moral subordination amongst men," so there should be princes and governors "to whom honor, subjection and obedience should be paid." Children were to be governed by parents, as "is most evidently founded in nature." God has appointed that there be moral rulers "that are the wiser and stronger" over the "less knowing and weaker." It logically followed for Edwards that the same pattern applied to the relation between mankind and God. "In maintaining communication or converse" between the two, "one must yield to the other, must comply with the other; there must be a union of wills; one must be clothed with authority, the other with submission."[73] Thus the chain of being put the stamp of approval upon the *status quo*, supporting a conservative moral and political outlook. There was to be no place for human pride or any tendency to move oneself from one's appointed station, and certainly there were no grounds for revolutionary action in the face of what obviously was the way God had created his world from top to bottom. Social relations were as much a part of the laws of nature as was nature itself.[74]

However, there was another aspect of this system that Arthur O. Lovejoy properly called the temporalizing of the chain. Movement by human beings was possible, as to their intelligence, will, and spiritual endowments. The conception of the destiny of man as an unending progress also entered the picture. Joseph Addison could claim "There is not . . . a more pleasing and triumphant consideration in religion than this of the perpetual progress which the soul makes towards the perfection of its nature, without ever arriving at a period in it . . . it must be a prospect pleasing to God himself, to see his creation ever beautifying in his eyes, and drawing nearer to him, by greater degrees of resemblance." And Leibniz concluded his *Principles of Nature and Grace* with the words that human happiness should consist "in a perpetual progress to new pleasures and perfections."[75]

These words could have been penned by Edwards, with one major exception. This lay in the fact that sin stood in the way, and by no amount of purely individual effort could one pass from sin to spiritual perfection. Furthermore, in Edwards's reading of it, the chain of being was less like a ladder to be climbed than a series of spiritual attainments to which one was lured by the beauty, power, and wisdom of God. The "climb," if that was what it was, was an ascent only for those who were saints, not an open invitation to natural human beings to strive to achieve their potentiality, as the Enlightenment moralists of the period supposed. But all else that the rationalistic purveyors of the chain-of-being philosophy claimed was acceptable to Edwards. There was to be for the saints, those endowed with true virtue, a never-ending progress of union with God in eternity, but they never would become God. The goal of unity with God and its blessedness could be approached or realized only asymptotically. "The time," Edwards wrote, "will never come when it can be said it is attained to, in the most absolutely perfect manner." Distance was still presupposed, in keeping with the principles of proportionality and hierarchy. Yet, "it is no solid objection against God's aiming at an infinitely perfect union of the creature with himself, that the particular time will never come when it can be said, the union is now infinitely perfect . . . there never will come the moment that now this infinitely valuable good has been actually bestowed."[76]

The metaphysical scene in which this portrayal of true virtue was set is one that takes the natural phenomena of the sun and a fountain to express the vital interchange between the saints and God. God, like a fountain or sun, overflows in His goodness and power, both creating the world and establishing the manner in which the saints will forever approach to a total union with Him. But for the word *creating* Edwards substituted the Neoplatonic term *emanation*. The relation of God to His world is not that of ruler exercising his sovereign rights over subjects so much as that of an infinitely fertile source of being and excellence that overflows into the world, filling the saints with His own nature, which is reflected back to Him. To the saints He communicates knowledge of Himself, which is "the image of God's own knowledge of himself." It is a participation in God as particular beams of the sun are communicated by the light and glory of that body. God emanates in an equally free-flowing manner His holiness, by which the creature partakes of God's own moral excellency. So the creature's holiness consists in love, which is the comprehension of all true virtue as it centers preeminently in God. "If holiness in God consist chiefly in love to himself, holiness in the creature must chiefly consist in love to him."[77] Then happiness comes, the happiness that

God has in Himself and His glory. This also is "something of God" in which the human subject is confirmed and united to God "in proportion as the communication is greater or less."[78]

All in all, the end for which the world was created is God's own glory. And that glory is "often represented by an effulgence, or emanation, or communication of light, from a luminary or fountain of light."[79] The saints' holiness or true virtue consists in their knowing, esteeming, loving, rejoicing in, and praising God, all of which is an exhibition of God's glory in them. So there is an interplay between the two. God's fullness is received by the saint and reflected back to the luminary, and this is emanation and remanation, as Edwards put it. True virtue is at last holiness, which is loving participation in the deity, whose glory is thereby manifested. God, it may be said, is the final lure that attracts the believer, whose will is determined by that which one loves. As he stated it in the "Freedom of the Will," "the will always *is* as the greatest apparent good, or as what appears most agreeable . . . ," and that is not to say that the will is under compulsion to love God, but rather is determined to love Him by the vision of the great Being.[80] One is irresistibly drawn to rest one's destiny in that which one loves above all else. Beyond that state of affairs, whereby God is glorified, no one can go.

Insofar as Edwards formulated his later conception of the saints' advance to true virtue and holiness on the model of the chain of being, he was using one that supposedly had been fashioned on the order of nature, although in fact its origin lay more in a metaphysical theory of nature than in an empirical view of it. Into that model the figures of the sun and fountain fitted as apt representations of the Neoplatonic tradition, although it was in significant ways different from the Newtonian world picture Edwards had developed earlier. Nevertheless, the pattern of nature found within the chain of being governed Edwards's way of describing how by degrees and proportionality true virtue came about. His aesthetic sensitivity to beauty in nature and his metaphysical ponderings on the ways of nature were translated to the higher plane of spiritual truth. It is no wonder that Edwards's more pedestrian critics found little by which to guide daily moral decisions in this transformation of ethics into holiness. True, in a certain way to guide one's steps by the principle of proportionality would curb the more extravagant exercises of self-interest, and conscience, implanted in all mankind "to be as it were in God's stead," could distinguish right from wrong, and might even put men "upon seeking true virtue."[81] But in the final analysis such secondary virtue could not of itself be lifted up to the breathless heights of holiness. Since true virtue was not simply a higher kind of morality on a scale of ethical achievement, it was an experience with which natural humanity was by and large unacquainted. It was a state of transformed consciousness and being that transcended the ethics of right and wrong and the demands of duty. It was an ecstasy, unachievable by human effort, that was intrinsically valuable and therefore useless as a means to anything beyond itself.

Nicolai Hartmann, although an atheist, has described such an experience as "radiant virtue," which flowed outward from the inherent richness of being in the human subject.[82] And Edwards's true virtue was precisely such a radiant virtue, given by God, of which morality as commonly understood was the most important by-product, but not the central point. Like Augustine's famous dictum, it was a matter of loving God and, from that source, doing what one wills.

6

Epilogue
Beyond the Valley in Fact and Symbol

It is generally agreed that location in a particular historical and cultural situation affects our thoughts and attitudes. I see no reason, by the same logic, to deny that one's placement in respect to nature may do the same. Physical height, for example, has almost universally been linked with a sense of superior value, and nowhere is this tendency more evident than in religion. Heights and mountains have long symbolized the divine. Gods are believed to inhabit high places, and the heavens bespeak the transcendence of things divine. The Bible expresses the importance of height as God manifests Himself on mountains, and sacred acts are performed in high places. God's omniscience, as He surveys all beneath him, is parallel to the synoptic vision an observer enjoys from a mountain.[1] Why should it not follow that human beings who live on or near mountains would be led to comprehensive and liberating ideas in opposition to all narrow and limited conceptions? Would not encompassing views from mountains give a sense of freedom that would break through the confines of earthbound perspectives? Undoubtedly life lived where vast stretches of the world below are viewed begets equally expansive feelings, but unfortunately for my theory, natural heights do not inevitably produce a liberality of viewpoint. When transferred to the mundane level, the comprehensiveness of mountain views is bought at the price of isolation from the concrete details that make up daily life. Height produces a sense of inclusive understanding and oceanic feelings, without which life would be the poorer, but the confusion and problems of a lower level demand more intimate and specific understandings and responses that narrow perspective. Breadth of vision gives way all too soon to ideas and attitudes rooted in the more constricted circumstances with which culture surrounds us and to which human nature condemns us.

Yet, we are not done with the theory that physical surroundings affect our thoughts and attitudes. If we take valleys instead of heights as our starting point, should we not assume that they limit ideas and feelings? Edwards, for example, was a son of the Connecticut Valley; did not the confines of the Valley circumscribe his ideas and religious outlook? True, he regarded mountains as types of heaven, but he also typified valleys as low places where waters run and collect, commonly signifying misery, "especially that which is occasioned by the wrath of God."[2] Valleys and the waters they contain may be symbols of condemnation and punishment, but that symbolism manifestly depends on the physical fact that valleys occur only in relation to the mountains that enclose them. Valleys by definition offer places of confinement, and therefore, in varying degrees, isolation. By only a short step one can see that geographical isolation leads to cultural isolation, with its attendant narrowness of insight. Was this not the very effect the Valley had on Edwards's mind?

We recall his boasting that the isolation of his part of the country protected it from the inroads of Arminianism, which flourished elsewhere in Massachusetts. Only a pathetically provincial thinker could have supposed, as did Edwards at the height of the awakenings, that the Kingdom of God was soon to appear on that little plot of land called New England. As a pastor his fretful nagging over tavern-haunting, frolics, and other enjoyable distractions, as well as his stubbornly clumsy handling of the "bad book" episode, mark him as a person busy with relatively tangential issues out of all proportion to their importance. Among his parishioners the bickerings over land and family prestige that helped to push him out of the pulpit were the sort of things to be expected in an isolated town bound up in its limited concerns. It can be suggested that Edwards's adherence to the confining tenets of Calvinism and his demand that strict limits be imposed on the conditions of admission for membership and communion in the church set him at odds with those of a more liberal turn of mind. Did not the insularity of the Valley engender those features of the Northampton scene, features that were not ameliorated but intensified by the isolation of his sojourn at Stockbridge in the Berkshire hills? Little wonder that to the popular mind Edwards comes down to us cast in the role of the prototypical, narrow-minded Puritan, hemmed in as much by his antiquated Calvinism as by geographical and cultural isolation. Ola E. Winslow credits Edwards with many virtues, but her biography of the man suggests that although these virtues were traceable "to the soil and society from which he came," in a measure "his intellectual blindness was traceable to the same sources."[3] This opinion, unfortunately, was based largely on her misunderstanding, if not distaste, for Edwards's Calvinism, which she regarded as already obsolete in his own time. Calvinist he undoubtedly was, but we often forget that Calvinism was a comprehensive intellectual and religious system with a universal appeal to cultured people who dared confront the tough realities of human existence. Edwards was one of these after his own kind.

Yes, I have made much of the fact that Edwards lived most of his life in the Valley, and have been quite ready to admit that in certain ways his geographical and cultural situation limited some options for his thought. What I have not established is any direct connection between his geographical situation and the quality or range of ideas that he in fact did hold. In that respect I have had little success in making nature, whether as valley or height, correlate with narrowness or liberality of mind. Rather, I am forced to admit that whatever physical limitations the Valley imposed upon him, they failed to dictate the heights, depth, or sweep of his ideas. Intellectually it was in the Valley that he coped with religious, scientific, and philosophical questions of universal significance, seemingly quite independent of his location. Those ideas and convictions culminated in treatises or works, some of which were completed at Stockbridge. Out of the revivals he helped to incite and of which he was a keen analyst and interpreter came his *Treatise Concerning Religious Affections*, one of the most searching expositions in defense of the role of emotions in religion ever penned. The threat of Arminianism, which he understood to be subverting the religious life of Western Massachusetts, inspired his great treatise on *The Freedom of the Will*, a work that continues to receive respectful philosophical attention even by those who would deny its religious or ethical applicability. In its companion piece, *The Great Christian Doctrine of Original Sin*, Edwards mounted a devastating attack upon the Pelagianism that was undercutting the orthodoxy he wished to defend. But it was a work that owed as much to his insights and readings on human nature as it did to his biblical and theological orthodoxy. The notes he left behind on science and metaphysics stemmed from his early Yale days. They largely came to an end after his arrival at Northampton, although there appear to have been occasional additions in Stockbridge as late as 1756 or 1757. Traces of these notes can be seen in many of his subsequent works. The "Miscellanies," begun during his brief stay in New York, were developed over the course of his life, and contain some of his most important observations on the mind and nature. From a series of sermons preached in 1739 Edwards planned to write a major treatise bearing the title *The History of the Work of Redemption*, a work that, if completed, would have surveyed God's work in respect to both nature and salvation history from creation to the end of time. His *Dissertation Concerning the End for which God Created the World* was a rehearsal of his favorite conviction of God's sovereignty, cast largely in Neoplatonic terms; in important ways it paved the way for his treatise on *The Nature of True Virtue*, as did also his earlier *Charity and its Fruits* and the *Religious Affections*. Unfortunately, the *True Virtue* remains an incomplete work. When these, out of many other writings are considered, it seems clear that his most fertile intellectual period occurred while he lived within the span of the Valley. However, in their range, taken collectively, they exhibit a mind that had risen above the provincialism often associated with valley experience. Perhaps had Edwards enjoyed a richer cultural milieu, his thoughts might have taken a different turn, but given the actual situation and the limited resources of the Yale education offered in his day, it is remarkable that he so far overcame the religious and intellectual obstacles they presented as to leave him symbolically well beyond the Valley's influence. His idea of God was far too great in majesty and beauty, whether cloaked in Calvinistic or Neoplatonic garb, to allow him to rest easy in any narrow, crabbed system. And in no small measure that expansiveness of thought was due to the play on his religious imagination of nature, seen as physical reality, symbol, or ideal construct. With the Bible and tradition, nature in one of its several forms paced alongside his first intimations of God's beauty and sovereignty, through *Religious Affections* and the theological and ethical heights of *God's End in Creation* and *True Virtue*. Nature, of course, was not the main focus of his spiritual and intellectual life. Nevertheless, the beauty and power of its physical presence impressed Edwards with spiritual graces and religious truth that opened his mind to realities beyond those transmitted to him by Scripture and tradition. As a rational system it discovered to him a manifestation of God's love of order that penetrated every aspect of the spiritual and moral life.

When physically he left the Valley for Stockbridge, he had long since departed from it intellectually and spiritually. Called from the isolation of Stockbridge to the presidency of the College of New Jersey, he soon died in Princeton of a smallpox inoculation, as has been mentioned, thus inadvertently proving the reality of physical matter that his metaphysics had explicitly denied. But death could not extinguish completely his vision of spiritual reality. His overwhelming sense of divine power and beauty, in spite of theological and metaphysical problems, remained a legacy for later generations.

That his most elevated and emancipative thoughts were to be encased in a forbiddingly rigid and austere system by his immediate successors was a misfortune for which he was only in part responsible.

If Edwards's immediate successors failed to exploit the spiritually emancipative aspects of their master's thought, later generations of commentators have been charged with too easily adapting him to the more expansive currents of modern thought foreign to his theological and cultural situation or further enclosing him in traditional categories of religious interpretation. The second and third generations of Edwardsean scholarship, it is alleged, reveal a series of conflicting polarities of interpretation based on assumptions and presuppositions, all of which should be called into question. Among the most familiar of these polar interpretations are those which see Edwards as either an incipient modernist or medievalist, Puritan or romantic, rationalist or mystic, empiricist or idealist. Recently R. C. DeProspo has called our attention to the inadequacy, if not the fruitlessness, of this struggle among the conflicting viewpoints that have marked the corpus of writings on Edwards. By the aid of authorities on phenomenology and the techniques of literary deconstruction, this scholar reassesses the historiography that has influenced most Edwardsean scholarship to date. He has discerned what he regards as a more inclusive polarity of interpretation by which, he claims, to "create" an Edwards who originates theistic discourse in distinction from that humanism by which some scholars have attempted to modernize Edwards.[4] However, the emphasis he gives to theistic discourse as a new and unique interpretive category strikes me as odd, since anyone familiar with Edwards's writings is already aware of the centrality of God in Edwards's life and thought. Having selected one among several possible definitions of theism that presumably are immune to further deconstruction, DeProspo offers a weighty study of how this type of discourse should influence interpretations of Edwards's thought and its effects on American culture.[5]

Certainly my present essay on Edwards's view of nature as sensately real, typologically instructive, and scientifically and metaphysically real in no way threatens theistic discourse, but it must be a discourse that proceeds in a more inclusive way than does that of DeProspo. The kind of theistic discourse I see in Edwards stems from the category of theological objectivism as set forth in my *The Ethics of Jonathan Edwards*.[6] The difference between DeProspo's conception of theistic discourse and my own lies in the fact that theological objectivism accommodates more than the Calvinist view of God as separate from the world, as DeProspo supposes to be the only form of theism Edwards held. Furthermore, instead of DeProspo's conception

of humanism in tension with theistic discourse, I employed subjec-
tivism and utilitarianism, that is, the focus on the human subject as
the counterpoise to theological objectivism.

   This thought experiment of mine places nature, an idea often over-
looked, denigrated, or extravagantly romanticized, in what I regard
as its rightful position in respect to Edwards's theistic discourse on
God, grace, faith, the religious affections, and true virtue. Of course
nature, as I have described it in these pages, was no substitute for
God, but it was an important and persisting aspect of Edwards's
theism and as such was often a controlling and structural feature of
these familiar patterns of religious thought. Whether I have made a
persuasive and intelligible case, others can judge, but as to whether
what I have written needs the ministration of deconstruction, as
apparently do all literary products on Edwards, I am supremely
indifferent.

Abbreviations

Many citations are designated in the notes by initials. For the convenience of the reader these are here listed alphabetically. For full description, see bibliography.

Primary Sources

AW	*Apocalyptic Writings*
CF	*Charity and Its Fruits*
CW	*Dissertation Concerning the End for which God Created the World*
DB	*The Life of David Brainerd*
Dw	*Memoir of his Life; Types of the Messiah and Notes on the Bible* (Sereno Dwight, ed.)
FS	*Forty Sermons on Various Subjects*
FW	*Freedom of the Will*
GA	*The Great Awakening*
He	*Treatise on Grace* and other posthumously published writings (Paul Helm, ed.)
HR	*A History of the Work of Redemption*
IS	*Images or Shadows of Divine Things*
MG	*God's Moral Government*
OS	*Original Sin*
RA	*Religious Affections*
SPW	*Scientific and Philosophical Writings*
To	*The Philosophy of Jonathan Edwards* (Harvey G. Townsend, ed.)
TV	*The Nature of True Virtue*

Secondary Sources

Fi   Norman Fiering, *Jonathan Edwards's Moral Thought and Its British Context*

Ho   Clyde A. Holbrook, *The Ethics of Jonathan Edwards*

Lo   Mason I. Lowance Jr., *The Language of Canaan*

Th   Keith Thomas, *Man and the Natural World*

Notes

Prologue

1. See the Reverend Theophilus Packard, Jr., *A History of the Churches and Ministers and of the Franklin Association in Franklin County* (Boston: S. F. Whipple and Co., 1854), 173–74; on Billings see Paul Jenkins, *The Conservative Rebel, A Social History of Greenfield, Massachusetts* (Town of Greenfield, Mass., 1982), 28–31.

2. Ola Elizabeth Winslow, *Jonathan Edwards* (New York: The Macmillan Co., 1941), 32.

3. Daniel B. Shea, Jr., "The Art and Instruction of Jonathan Edwards' 'Personal Narrative,'" in *The American Puritan Imagination*, ed. Sacvan Bercovitch (Cambridge: Cambridge University Press, 1974), 159. See also R. C. DeProspo, *Theism in the Discourse of Jonathan Edwards* (Newark: University of Delaware Press; London and Toronto, Associated University Presses, 1985). Edwards "studies the natural world only to the degree that he thinks it manifests the design of its Creator . . . natural man and his natural environment seldom interest Edwards intrinsically," 58.

Chapter 1. The Valley and Nature at First Hand

1. Th. 259.

2. Cf. SPW 238–39, no.45.

3. Cf. IS 75–77, no. 77.

4. Cited in Peter N. Carroll, *Puritanism and the Wilderness* (New York and London: Columbia University Press, 1969), 111; henceforth cited as Carroll.

5. Cf. Alan Heimert, "The Wilderness and the Frontier," *The New England Quarterly* 36, no. 3 (September 1953): 377, 373.

6. Cf. Carroll, 120, 185.

7. Cf. ibid., 122, 124.

8. See Patricia J. Tracy, *Jonathan Edwards Pastor: Religion and Society in Eighteenth Century Northampton* (New York: Hill and Wang, 1980), 38 ff.

9. GA 356.

10. Cf. Dw 1:12, 9.

11. Cf. ibid., 603.

12. Ibid., 109.

13. Cf. GA 144–46.

14. Cf. Ibid., 562–63; cf. Paul R. Lucas, *Valley of Discord* (Hanover, N.H.: The University Press of New England, 1976), chap. 7.

15. See map in Edwin Scott Gaustad, *The Great Awakening in New England* (New York: Harper and Brothers, 1956), facing 24, or GA map, p.24.

16. Dw 1:555.

17. Cf. "Some Old Letters Relating to Early Stockbridge, 1749–1754." Reprint from Scribner's Magazine (February 1895), 3,4,7,9,16.

18. *The New England Quarterly* 11 (1968): 95; see DeProspro for contrary opinion, 177.

19. Cf. Dw 1:59.

20. Cf. Ibid., 61–62.

21. Cf. Ibid., 66,67.

22. Cf. Ibid., 84,85.

23. Cf. Ibid., 133.

24. Ibid., 115.

25. RA 374.

26. Cf. Th 216, 249, 213.

27. SPW 242.

28. GA 195.

29. SPW 353, no. 34.

30. Cf. Robert Daly, *God's Altar* (Berkeley, Los Angeles, London: University of California Press, 1978), 8–9.

31. Dw 1:65.

32. Cf., e.g., Richard S. Westfall, *Science and Religion in Seventeenth Century England* (New Haven: Yale University Press, 1958), chaps. 1, 2.

33. Cf. SPW 6.

34. Cf. Dw 1:28, 254.

35. Cf. SPW 147, 150.

36. Ibid., 194, no. 16.

37. Dw 1:569.

38. Cf. SPW 154–55.

39. Cf. ibid., 158.

40. Cf. ibid., 161, 163.

41. Th 173.

42. Ibid., 278.

43. Ibid., 278–79.

44. Cf. SPW 161, cors. 1 and 2.

45. Cf. ibid., 51.

46. Cf. Th 176, 19, 22;138, 20, 21.

47. To 237, ll; description of "Miscellanies" see To xvi–xviii.

48. Cf. SPW 373–75.

49. Cf. *Book of Controversies*, MS. 28, 181, paras. 3 and 4, Beinecke Rare Book and Manuscript Library, Yale University.

50. RA 296–97.

51. Cf. SPW 15, 119–20, no. 16.

52. Cited in ibid., 35.

53. Dw 1:79.

54. Ibid., 80.

55. Cf. ibid., 81,82.

56. Ibid.

57. Ibid., 83.

58. Ibid., 104.

59. Ibid., 107.

60. Cf. ibid., 133.

61. Cf. ibid., 544.
62. Cf. ibid., 546.
63. Cf. ibid., 568.
64. CF 489.
65. Cf. GA 300–303; 443–44.
66. Cf. RA 98.
67. SPW 339. no. 4.
68. Ibid., 246, no. 51.

Chapter 2. Nature at Second Hand

1. In He 128–29.
2. Cf., e.g., DB 23; Terrence Erdt, *Jonathan Edwards' Art and the Sense of the Heart* (Amherst: University of Massachusetts Press, 1980), 49–50.
3. Cf. SPW 241–42.
4. Cf. ibid., 236, no. 31.
5. Cf., e.g., ibid., 307–10.
6. Cf. ibid., 397.
7. Cf. ibid., 302–4.
8. Ibid., 353, no. 34.
9. Cf. GA 331 ff.
10. Cf. RA 199 ff.
11. Cf. To xvii.
12. See Christopher Hill, "Science in Seventeenth-Century England," *The BBC Listener*, 7 June 1962.
13. Cf. Richard S. Westfall, *Science and Religion in Seventeenth Century England* (New Haven: Yale University Press, 1958), 9 ff.
14. In ibid. 23.
15. "Living Things in the Frame of Nature," *The BBC Listener*, 13 August 1959, 241.
16. Cf. SPW 38,39.
17. Cf. ibid., 265, no. 6.
18. To 184–85, Misc. 1263.
19. Cf. ibid., 191.
20. Ibid., 191, 192–93.
21. Cf. CW 202, 255.
22. Cf. Basil Willey, *The Eighteenth Century Background* (London: Chatto and Windus, 1946), 29.
23. Cf. David R. Williams, "This Consciousness That Is Aware—Emily Dickinson in the Wilderness of the Mind," in *Soundings* 66, no. 3 (Fall 1983): 371.
24. SPW 216, cor. 15.
25. To 261–62, Misc. 651.
26. Cf. ibid., 235, no. 26, 53–54 ff.
27. Ibid., 216, cor. 16.
28. Cf. ibid., 62.
29. *Essay on Human Understanding*, ed. Alexander Campbell Fraser (New York: Dover, 1954), 464, no. 23.
30. Cf. G. J. Warnock, *Berkeley* (Baltimore, Md.: Penguin Books, 1969), 22; G. R. Cragg, *Reason and Authority in the Eighteenth Century*, (Cambridge: Cambridge University Press, 1964), 98 ff.
31. Cf. SPW 63.

32. Cf. ibid., 215, cor. 11.
33. Cf. ibid., 380 no. 61.
34. Cf. ibid., 215, cor. 11.
35. OS 398–401.
36. Cf. Clyde A. Holbrook, "Jonathan Edwards on Self-Identity and Original Sin," *The Eighteenth Century* 25, no. 1 (1984): 55–56.
37. To 76, no. 125.
38. SPW 67.
39. Ibid., 235, no. 26.
40. To 129, Misc. 247.
41. SPW 238, cor. 3.
42. Ibid., 206, cor. 1
43. Cf. ibid., 342, 344–45, cor. 15.
44. Cf. Warnock, 89.
45. SPW 340, no. 6.
46. Cf. ibid., 344–45, no. 15.
47. *Process and Reality*, ed. David Ray Griffin and Donald W. Sherburne (New York: The Free Press, 1978), 346–47.
48. Cf. TV 9n.
49. Cf. SPW 206, cor. 1.
50. Ibid., no. 16.
51. Cf. ibid., 305–6.
52. Cf. ibid., 307–10.
53. Ibid., 335.
54. Cf. ibid., 342, no. 11; 385–86, no. 72; OS 398–406.
55. SPW 357–58; FW 392–93.
56. Cf. ibid., 231, no. 14.
57. Ibid., no. 17.
58. Cf. Fi 78, 70–71.
59. Cf., e.g., SPW 356, no. 40; 232, no. 20; 278, no. 14; 286, no. 25.
60. Ibid., 335.
61. To 258, Misc. 117; SPW 337.
62. SPW 363.
63. CW 257; cf. Ho 111–12.
64. SPW 381.
65. To 183.
66. Cf. SPW 336.
67. Cf. ibid., 382, no. 63.
68. Ibid., 380, no. 62.
69. Ibid., 382, no. 63.
70. Cf. ibid., 362, no. 45.
71. Cf. ibid., 333, 334.
72. Cf. ibid., 332–36.
73. Ibid., 265, no. 5.
74. Ibid., 81.
75. Cf. RA 147, no. 7; 365, no. x; also GA 307, 463–66, 470, 510, 522.
76. SPW 381.
77. Cf. Joseph Butler, *The Analogy of Religion* (New York: Robert Carter and Brothers, n.d.), xlviii–xlix, li.
78. Cf. SPW 349, no. 23.
79. To 262, no. 651.

80. SPW 391, no. 36.
81. Cf. OS 406–7.
82. Cited in IS 131.
83. Cf. Fi 84–85.
84. George S. Hendry, *The Theology of Nature* (Philadelphia: The Westminster Press, 1980), 62.
85. To 238, no. 42.
86. To 236–37 gg.
87. Cf. To 263–68, 136, 215 (Schafer transcript), Misc. 725, 867, 990, 1038, 1041, 547.
88. Ibid., 237.
89. Cf. SPW 242 ff., no. 48.
90. Ibid., 231, no. 16.
91. Gerald R. Cragg, *Reason and Authority in the Eighteenth Century* (Cambridge: Cambridge University Press, 1964), 8.

Chapter 3. The Ambiguities of Nature

1. Cf. Alfred North Whitehead, *Science and the Modern World* (New York: The Free Press, 1953), 54–55.
2. In *Alfred North Whitehead, an Anthology*, selected by F. C. S. Northrup and Mason W. Gross (New York: The Macmillan Co., 1953), 338.
3. Cf. R. G. Collingwood, *The Idea of Nature* (Oxford: Clarendon Press, 1945), 113–14; also SPW 36, 102–3, 123–24.
4. Cf. Émile Bréhier, *Histoire de la Philosophie*, vol. 2, sec. 2 (Paris: Presses Universitaires de France, 1962), 361.
5. IS 140 n. 21.
6. Wallace E. Anderson, "Immaterialism in Jonathan Edwards' Early Philosophical Notes," *Journal of the History of Ideas* 25 (1964): 181. See also To vi.
7. Cf. SPW 36, 123, 372 n. 1.
8. "The 'Idealism' of Jonathan Edwards," *Harvard Theological Review* 62 (1964): 211.
9. Bréhier, *Histoire*, 2:347.
10. Cf. SPW 102–3, 112.
11. Cf. Bruce Kuklick, *Churchmen and Philosophers* (New Haven and London: Yale University Press, 1985), 18–19.
12. SPW 398.
13. Cf. ibid., 353, no. 34.
14. Cf. ibid., 368, no. 5.
15. Ibid., 363, no. 8.
16. To 74.
17. SPW 202, 206.
18. Ibid., 350, no. 26.
19. Cf. FW 34–37, 180–81, 264–65.
20. Cf. Bertrand Russell, *A History of Western Philosophy* (London: Allen and Unwin Ltd., 1948), 674, 677–78.
21. Cf. SPW 350–51, no. 27.
22. Ibid., 204–5.
23. Cf. ibid., 214, cor. 6.
24. Ibid., 335.
25. Ibid., 337

26. Cf. Arthur O. Lovejoy, *The Great Chain of Being* (Cambridge, Mass.: Harvard University Press, 1942), 30–31.

27. Cf. SPW 347.

28. Cf. RA 288.

29. SPW 246, no. 51

30. To 236, Misc. gg.

31. Cf. ibid., 136, Misc. 547, cor. 2.

32. Cf. SPW 354–55.

33. To 237, Misc. ll.

34. Cf. SPW 347.

35. Cf. ibid., 351, no. 27; 356, n. 40.

36. Ibid., 206, cor. 1.

37. Ibid., 205.

38. Cf. ibid., 241, no. 47.

39. Ibid., 398.

40. Ibid., 235, no. 26.

41. Cf. To 128, Misc. 247.

42. Cf. G. J. Warnock, *Berkeley* (Baltimore, Md.: Penguin Books, 1964), 9.

43. Cf. SPW 103.

44. Ibid., 353, no. 34.

45. Ibid.

46. Cf. *Jonathan Edwards, Selections*, ed. Clarence H. Faust and Thomas H. Johnson, rev. ed. (New York: Hill and Wang, 1965), xxviii.

47. Cf. SPW 36, 37, 395.

48. Ibid., 156.

49. Cf. ibid., 352–53, no. 31.

50. Ibid., 355, no. 35.

51. To 223, Misc. 1340.

52. SPW 359, cor. 40.

53. Ibid., 107.

54. Ibid., 357.

55. Ibid., 368, no. 51.

56. Ibid., 109.

57. Ibid., 345, no. 15; 342, no. 10.

58. Ibid. 246, no. 50.

59. Ibid., 283, no. 21.

60. Ibid., 246, no. 51.

61. Ibid., 347, 348, no. 21a.

62. Ibid., 379, no. 43.

63. Cf. ibid., 358–59, no. 40; 105.

64. RA 98.

65. Ibid., 344, no. 13; 359, no. 51.

66. Cf. Ian G. Barbour, *Issues in Science and Religion* (Englewood Cliffs, N.J.: Prentice-Hall, Inc., 1966), 26–27, 34–35.

67. Perry Miller, *Jonathan Edwards* (New York: Meridian Books, 1959), 89–90.

68. SPW, 351.

69. Ibid., 212.

70. Ibid., 351.

71. Cf. ibid., 98.

72. Cf. ibid., 214–15.

73. Ibid., 353, no. 34.

74. Ibid., 348, no. 22

75. Cf. ibid., 359, no. 41.
76. Cf. ibid., 361, cor. 43; 391–92, no. 43.
77. To 74, Misc. pp.
78. Cf. He 100–101, 103, 104, 130.
79. Cf. ibid., 90.
80. FS 4:186–90; also 362, 430, 433.
81. SPW, 238, cor. 3.
82. Ibid., 396.
83. Cf. ibid., 349, no. 23.
84. TV 64.
85. Cf. ibid., 30.
86. Fi 118.

Chapter 4. Nature and History in Symbolic Guise

1. SPW 361, no. 43.
2. Cf. "Note on Types," Andover Library. I am indebted to Ruth Mastin Anderson for this and the following reference from Wallace E. Anderson's material on "Types."
3. Ibid.
4. Dw 9:110.
5. IS 41.
6. Cf. ibid., 8.
7. Cf. Dw 9:28.
8. Cf. G. W. H. Lampe and K. J. Woolcombe, *Essays on Typology* (Naperville, Ill.: Alec R. Allenson, Inc., 1957), 9–14; IS 8–17; cf. Conrad Cherry, *Nature and Religious Imagination* (Philadelphia, Fortress Press, 1980), chaps. 1 and 2.
9. Cf. AW 1.
10. IS 28, 29.
11. Ibid., 36.
12. Ibid., 109, no. 156.
13. Ibid., 19–20.
14. In Mason I. Lowance Jr., in *Literary Uses of Typology*, ed. Earl Miner (Princeton, N.J.: Princeton University Press, 1977), 265.
15. IS 91, no. 109; 93, no. 116; Perry Miller, *The New England Mind* (New York: The Macmillan Co., 1939), 213–14.
16. Cf. IS 93, no. 113.
17. Cf. ibid., 25, 27.
18. He 127.
19. HR 394.
20. Cf. Dw 9:2–3.
21. IS 46, no. 22; cf. Cherry, 9–10.
22. Cf. IS 1–2.
23. Lo 261.
24. Cf. Misc 362 in Lo 263.
25. Misc. 638, IS 27.
26. Cf. IS 45, no. 10.
27. Ibid. 97, no. 128.
28. Ibid.
29. Ibid., 67, no. 64.
30. Dw 9: 176.
31. AW 165.

32. Cf. Ibid., 124.
33. Cf. IS 94, no. 116.
34. Cf. ibid., 91, no. 109; 93, no. 115.
35. Cf. ibid., 43, no. 3.
36. Cf. ibid., 48, no. 24.
37. Cf. ibid., 57, no. 47.
38. Cf. AW 115.
39. Cf. IS 75–77, no. 77; HR 511.
40. Ibid., 134, no. 212; 47, no. 21.
41. Cf. ibid., 79, no. 79.
42. Cf. ibid., 59, no. 53.
43. Cf. ibid., 79, no. 80.
44. Cf. ibid., 38, no. 97.
45. Cf. ibid., 61, no. 58; He 127; cf. R. C. DeProspo, *Theism in the Discourse of Jonathan Edwards* (Newark: University of Delaware Press, 1985), 173–74.
46. Cf. SPW 298–302.
47. Cf. also AW 108, where the stars are the visible saints, reflecting Christ's light.
48. Cf. also IS 61–64, no. 58.
49. Cf. Dw 9:181–86.
50. Cf. IS 6–7.
51. Cf. SPW 229 ff., nos. 1–5, 247, no. 54.
52. AW 140. Misc. 149 even depicts the saints as having beautiful bodies of "charming proportions" in the "new Jerusalem." (Schafer transcript)
53. Cf. To 263–68.
54. Cf. AW 140–42, 158, 166.
55. Cf. SPW 373–75, no. 59; IS 46–47, no. 19.
56. Cf. Charles E. Raven, *Natural Religion and Christian Theology*, 1st ser.: *Science and Religion* (Cambridge: Cambridge University Press, 1953), 54–57; cf. also Mary B. Hesse, *Science and the Human Imagination* (London: SCM Ltd., 1954), 20.
57. Cf. Th 105 ff.
58. Cf. SPW 224, no. 22.
59. Ibid., 223, no. 19; 228–29, no. 28.
60. IS 122, no. 174.
61. Ibid., 50, no. 35; 101, nos. 142, 144.
62. Ibid., 129, no. 198.
63. Cf. ibid., 82, no. 82.
64. Cf. ibid., 92, no. 110.
65. Cf. ibid., 96, no. 125.
66. Ibid., 45, no. 11; 66, no. 63.
67. Ibid., 124, no. 181.
68. Ibid., 97, no. 127.
69. Cf. ibid., 110, no. 160.
70. Ibid., 65, no. 61.
71. Cf. ibid., 182, no. 204.
72. Ibid., 134, no. 211.
73. Ibid., 98, no. 137.
74. Ibid., 122, no. 177.
75. Ibid., 98, no. 133.
76. Ibid., 105, no. 153.
77. Ibid., 102, no. 148.
78. Ibid., 122, no. 176.
79. Ibid., 123, no. 179.

80. Dw ix, 179.
81. Cf. "The Excellency of Christ," FS 4 : 179–80.
82. Cf. Dw 9 : 118.
83. Cf. ibid., 119.
84. Cf. ibid., 122–24.
85. Cf. ibid., 130–32.
86. Cf. ibid., 142–43, 145.
87. Cf. ibid., 172–73.
88. Cf., e.g., ibid., 43–86.
89. Cf. ibid., 19, 21.
90. Ibid., 108–9.
91. Cf. ibid., 97 ff.
92. Cf. ibid., 462–63.
93. Cf. ibid., 221.
94. Cf. ibid., 186–210.
95. Cf. ibid., 28.
96. Dw 1 : 569–70.
97. Cf. HR 300.
98. Beinecke Rare Book and Manuscript Library, Yale University.
99. RA 288.
100. HR 315.
101. Ibid., 494.
102. Ibid., 303.
103. Cf. To 263 ff.; Misc. 867, 990.
104. Ibid., 516.
105. Cf. SPW 204, 368, no. 51.
106. Cf. SPW 353, no. 34.
107. Cf. Bruce Kuklick, *Churchmen and Philosophers* (New Haven and London: Yale University Press, 1985), 23, 28.
108. Cf. SPW 37.
109. Dw 9 : 172.
110. Ibid., 447 (erroneously paged as 467).
111. Ibid., 462.
112. Cf. HR 324 ff., 355–70.
113. Cf. AW 98–99.
114. Cf. ibid., 110.
115. Cf. ibid., 113.
116. Cf. ibid., 110.
117. Cf. ibid., 185.
118. Cf. ibid., 195.
119. Cf. Dw 9 : 110.
120. Ibid., 110.
121. G. W. H. Lampe and K. J. Woolcombe, *Essays on Typology* (Naperville) 14. On the conflict between a literal or historical reading of biblical texts and figurative language, see Hans Frei, *The Eclipse of Biblical Narrative* (New Haven and London: Yale University Press, 1974), 2, 6–7, 12, 27–30.
122. IS 131, no. 203.
123. Ibid., 65, no. 59.
124. SPW 335.
125. Ibid.
126. Cf. IS 79, no. 79.
127. SPW 391, no. 36.

128. In Lo 251. Cf. Frei, intro. and chap. 1.

129. IS 69–70, no. 70.

130. Lo 273, 6–8.

131. Cf. RA 266.

132. Ibid., 283. Edwards was unclear as to the meaning and use of the new sense of the heart." See Stephen J. Stein, "The Quest for the Spiritual Sense: The Biblical Hermeneutics of Jonathan Edwards," in *Harvard Theological Review* 70 (January–April 1977): 109 ff.

133. Paul Helm, "John Locke and Jonathan Edwards: a Reconsideration," *Journal of the History of Philosophy* 7 (1969): 54.

134. Fi 125; cf. Terrence Erdt, *Jonathan Edwards, Art and the Sense of the Heart* (Amherst: University of Massachusetts Press, 1980), 1–4.

135. Cf. Clyde A. Holbrook, "Jonathan Edwards on Self-Identity and Original Sin," *The Eighteenth Century* 25, no. 1 (1984): 44 ff.

136. RA 460.

Chapter 5. Nature, Morality, and Holiness

1. TV 64.

2. Earl R. Wasserman, "Nature Moralized: The Divine Analogy in the Eighteenth Century," *ELH, A Journal of English Literary History*, no. 20 (March 1953), 1, 51, 57, 61.

3. Cf., e.g., SPW 231, no. 16; 236, nos. 31, 36; 248, no. 55.

4. Cf. To 27.

5. Cf. ibid., 261–62, Misc. 651.

6. TV 3–4.

7. SPW 362, no. 45.

8. Cf. ibid., 305–6.

9. Ibid., 335; cf. also 344.

10. Cf. ibid., 380, no. 62.

11. Fi 84–85.

12. Cf. SPW 235, no. 23b; 357, no. 40.

13. Cf. ibid., 343.

14. Ibid., 336.

15. Ibid., 380, no. 62; cf. 382, no. 62.

16. Cf. ibid., 381, no. 62.

17. Cf. ibid., 363–64, nos. 4, 9.

18. Cf. To 258, Misc. 117; TV 23; SPW 337.

19. Cf. He 99.

20. TV 9.

21. Cf. CW 201, 203.

22. CF 479–85. Cf. Misc. 369, 403, 431, 681, 817, 822 on degrees and proportions of saints' glory and happiness. (Schafer transcript)

23. SPW 336.

24. GA 470.

25. Cf. TV 12.

26. Cf. CF 479, 482, 485.

27. Cf. ibid., 145, 150–51.

28. TV 3.

29. Cf. SPW 381.

30. Cf. TV 5.

31. TV 38.

32. Ibid., 6.

33. SPW 381.

34. Cf. The Reverend William Hart, *Remarks on President Edwards's Dissertation Concerning the Nature of True Virtue* (New Haven, Conn.: T. and S. Green, 1771), 4.

35. Cf. Robert Hall, *Works in Four Volumes* (New York: Harper and Brothers, 1849), 1:43. Hall was a prominent Baptist preacher in England, 1764–1831. Cf. Ho 123–25.

36. Cf. CW 215.

37. TV 9.

38. CW 255.

39. Cf. SPW 202, 206.

40. Cf. Douglas J. Elwood, *The Philosophical Theology of Jonathan Edwards* (New York: Columbia University Press, 1961), 29; Joseph Haroutunian, *Piety Versus Moralism* (New York: Henry Holt and Co., 1932), 78.

41. Cf. SPW 337.

42. Cf. ibid., 381, no. 62.

43. Cf. TV 28.

44. Ibid., 31.

45. Ibid., 35.

46. Cf. Roland Delattre, *Beauty and Sensibility in the Thought of Jonathan Edwards* (New Haven: Yale University Press, 1968), 9, 18, 20, 23, 24, 26.

47. OS 141.

48. RA 240.

49. TV 8, 14.

50. CF 227.

51. Cf. TV 4, 5.

52. Cf. To 21–25. On the question of whether in the eighteenth century harmony in music immediately pleases, see John Neubauer, *The Emancipation of Music from Language* (New Haven and London: Yale University Press, 1986), esp. 160, 175–76, 178, 179.

53. Ho 206, n. 12; 207, n. 17; 209, n. 35.

54. Cf. Fi 81.

55. TV 98–99.

56. Cf. ibid., 33.

57. Cf. ibid., 32, 40, 41.

58. To 205, no. 7 39.

59. Cf. ibid., 16–17, 26; Ho 102.

60. Cf. To 147–48, cor. 1.

61. TV 51; for other criticisms by Edwards of the moral-sense philosophers, see ibid., 48–60.

62. Cf. ibid., 70.

63. Ibid., 22.

64. Ibid., 87.

65. Cf. ibid., 57, 89.

66. Cf. CF 284.

67. Cf. GA 470.

68. Cf. TV 47–48.

69. Ibid., 30.

70. Ibid., 68.

71. Ibid., 40–41.

72. Cf. RA 266.

73. Cf. MG 566–72.

74. Cf. Gerald R. Cragg, *Puritanism in the Period of the Great Persecution, 1660–1688* (Cambridge: Cambridge University Press, 1957), 230.

75. In Arthur O. Lovejoy, *The Great Chain of Being* (Cambridge, Mass.: Harvard University Press, 1942), 247, 248.

76. CW 257.

77. Ibid., 217.

78. Ibid., 210–11.

79. Ibid., 250.

80. FW 144, 12.

81. TV 90, 853.

82. Nicolai Hartmann, *Ethics*, (London: George Allen and Unwin; New York, The Macmillan Co., 1932), 2:332–38.

Chapter 6. Epilogue

1. Cf. Clyde A. Holbrook, *The Iconoclastic Deity* (Lewisburg, Pa.: Bucknell University Press, 1984), 199–200, 209–10.

2. IS 67, no. 63.

3. Ola Elizabeth Winslow, *Jonathan Edwards* (New York: The Macmillan Co., 1941), 327.

4. Cf. DeProspo, *Theism*, 10, chap. 5.

5. Cf. ibid., 12–13.

6. Cf. Ho chaps. 1, 2.

Bibliography

Works by Jonathan Edwards

Apocalyptic Writings. Works of Jonathan Edwards, vol. 5. Edited by Stephen J. Stein. New Haven and London: Yale University Press, 1977. (AW)

Charity and Its Fruits. Edited by Tryon Edwards. New York: Robert Carter and Brothers, 1852. (CF)

Dissertation Concerning the End for which God Created the World. The Works of President Edwards in Four Volumes, A Reprint of the Worcester Edition, vol. 2. New York: Leavitt and Allen, 1843.(CW)

Forty Sermons on Various Subjects. The Works of President Edwards in Four Volumes, A Reprint of the Worcester Edition, vol. 4. New York: Leavitt and Allen, 1843. (FS)

Freedom of the Will. Works of Jonathan Edwards, vol. 1. Edited by Paul Ramsey. New Haven: Yale University Press; London: Oxford University Press, 1957. (FW)

God's Moral Government. The Works of President Edwards in Four Volumes, A Reprint of the Worcester Edition, vol. 1. New York: Leavitt and Allen, 1843.(MG)

The Great Awakening. Works of Jonathan Edwards, vol. 4. Edited by C. C. Goen. New Haven and London: Yale University Press, 1972. (GA)

A History of the Work of Redemption. The Works of President Edwards in Four Volumes, A Reprint of the Worcester Edition, vol. 1. New York: Leavitt and Allen, 1943. (HR)

Images or Shadows of Divine Things. Edited by Perry Miller. New Haven: Yale University Press; London: Geoffrey Cumberledge, Oxford University Press, 1948. (IS)

Jonathan Edwards, Selections. Edited by Clarence H. Faust and Thomas H. Johnson. rev. ed. New York: Hill and Wang, 1965.

The Life of David Brainerd. Works of Jonathan Edwards, vol. 7. Edited by Norman Pettit. New Haven and London: Yale University Press, 1985. (DB)

Memoirs of His Life. The Works of President Edwards with a Memoir of His Life in Ten Volumes, vol. 1. New York: Published by S. Converse, 1829. Known as the Dwight Edition. (Dw)

The Nature of True Virtue. Foreword by William K. Frankena. Ann Arbor Paperbacks. Ann Arbor: University of Michigan Press, 1960. (TV)

Original Sin. Works of Jonathan Edwards, vol. 3. Edited by Clyde A. Holbrook. New Haven and London: Yale University Press, 1970. (OS)

The Philosophy of Jonathan Edwards. Edited by Harvey G. Townsend. Eugene: University of Oregon Press, 1958. (To)

Religious Affections. Works of Jonathan Edwards, vol. 2. Edited by John E. Smith. New Haven and London: Yale University Press, 1959. (RA)

Scientific and Philosophical Writings. Works of Jonathan Edwards, vol. 6. Edited by Wallace E. Anderson. New Haven and London: Yale University Press, 1980. (SPW)

Treatise on Grace and other posthumously published writings. Edited by Paul Helm. Cambridge and London: James Clarke and Co., Ltd., 1971. (He)

Types of the Messiah and Notes on the Bible. The Works of President Edwards with a Memoir of His Life in Ten Volumes, vol. 9. New York: G. and C. and H. Carvill, 1830. Known as the Dwight edition. (Dw)

Secondary Sources

Barbour, Ian G. *Issues in Science and Religion*. Englewood Cliffs, N. J.: Prentice-Hall, Inc., 1966.

Bréhier, Émile. *Histoire de la Philosophie*. vol. 2, sec. 2. Paris: Presses Universitaires de France, 1962.

Butler, Joseph. *The Analogy of Religion*. New York: Robert Carter and Brothers, n.d.

Carroll, Peter N. *Puritanism and the Wilderness*. New York and London: Columbia University Press, 1969.

Cherry, Conrad. *Nature and Religious Imagination*. Philadelphia: Fortress Press, 1980.

Collingwood, R. G. *The Idea of Nature*. Oxford: The Clarendon Press, 1945.

Cragg, Gerald R. *Puritanism in the Period of the Great Persecution, 1660–1688*. Cambridge: Cambridge University Press, 1957.

―――. *Reason and Authority in the Eighteenth Century*. Cambridge: Cambridge University Press, 1964.

Daly, Robert. *God's Altar.* Berkeley, Los Angeles, London: University of California Press, 1978.

Delattre, Roland. *Beauty and Sensibility in the Thought of Jonathan Edwards.* New Haven: Yale University Press, 1968.

DeProspo, R. C. *Theism in the Discourse of Jonathan Edwards.* Newark: University of Delaware Press; London and Toronto, Associated University Presses, 1985.

Elwood, Douglas J. *The Philosophical Theology of Jonathan Edwards.* New York: Columbia University Press, 1961.

Erdt, Terrence. *Jonathan Edwards' Art and the Sense of the Heart.* Amherst, Mass., University of Massachusetts Press, 1980.

Fiering, Norman. *Jonathan Edwards's Moral Thought and Its British Context.* Chapel Hill: The University of North Carolina Press, 1981. (Fi)

Frei, Hans. *The Eclipse of Biblical Narrative.* New Haven and London: Yale University Press, 1974.

Gaustad, Edwin Scott. *The Great Awakening in New England.* New York: Harper and Brothers, 1956.

Hall, Robert. *Works in Four Volumes.* New York: Harper and Brothers, 1849.

Hart, William. *Remarks on President Edwards's Dissertation Concerning the Nature of True Virtue.* New Haven: T. and S. Green, 1771.

Hartmann, Nicolai. *Ethics.* 3 vols. London: George Allen and Unwin; New York: The Macmillan Co., 1932.

Hendry, George S. *The Theology of Nature.* Philadelphia: The Westminster Press, 1980.

Hesse, Mary B. *Science and the Human Imagination.* London: SCM Press, Ltd., 1954.

Holbrook, Clyde A. *The Ethics of Jonathan Edwards.* Ann Arbor: University of Michigan Press, 1973. (Ho)

―――. *The Iconoclastic Deity.* Lewisburg, Pa.: Bucknell University Press, 1984.

Jenkins, Paul. *The Conservative Rebel, A Social History of Greenfield, Massachusetts.* Published by the Town of Greenfield, Massachusetts, 1982.

Kuklick, Bruce. *Churchmen and Philosophers.* New Haven and London: Yale University Press, 1985.

Lampe, G. W. H., and H. J. Woolcombe. *Essays on Typology.* Naperville, Ill.: Alec R. Allenson, Inc., 1957.

Locke, John. *Essay on Human Understanding.* Edited by Alexander Campbell Fraser. New York: Dover, 1954.

Lovejoy, Arthur O. *The Great Chain of Being*. Cambridge, Mass.: Harvard University Press, 1942.

Lowance, Mason I., Jr. *The Language of Canaan*. Cambridge, Mass. and London: Harvard University Press, 1980. (Lo)

Lucas, Paul R. *Valley of Discord*. Hanover, N.H.: The University Press of New England, 1976.

Miller, Perry, *Jonathan Edwards*. New York: Meridian Books, 1959.

——. *The New England Mind*. New York: The Macmillan Co., 1939.

Miner, Earl, ed. *Literary Uses of Typology*. Princeton: Princeton University Press, 1977.

Neubauer, John. *The Emancipation of Music from Language*. New Haven and London: Yale University Press, 1986.

Packard, Theophilus, Jr. *A History of the Churches and Ministers and of the Franklin Association in Franklin County*. Boston: S. V. Whipple and Co., 1854.

Russell, Bertrand. *A History of Western Philosophy*. London: Allen and Unwin Ltd., 1948.

Shea, Samuel B., Jr. "The Art and Instruction of Jonathan Edwards' 'Personal Narrative.'" In *The American Puritan Imagination*, edited by Sacvan Bercovitch. Cambridge: Cambridge University Press, 1974.

Thomas, Keith. *Man and the Natural World*. New York: Pantheon Press, 1983. (Th)

Tracy, Patricia J. *Jonathan Edwards Pastor: Religion and Society in Eighteenth Century Northampton*. New York: Hill and Wang, 1980.

Warnock, G. J. *Berkeley*. Baltimore, Md.: Penguin Books, 1969.

Westfall, Richard S. *Science and Religion in Seventeenth Century England*. New Haven: Yale University Press, 1958.

Whitehead, Alfred North. *Alfred North Whitehead, an Anthology*. Selected by F. C. S. Northrop and Mason W. Gross. New York: The Macmillan Co., 1953.

——. *Process and Reality*. Edited by David Ray Griffin and Donald W. Sherburne. New York: The Free Press, 1978.

——. *Science and the Modern World*. New York: The Free Press, 1953.

Willey, Basil. *The Eighteenth Century Background*. London: Chatto and Windus, 1946.

Winslow, Ola Elizabeth. *Jonathan Edwards*. New York: The Macmillan Co., 1941.

Periodical Articles

Anderson, Wallace C. "Immaterialism in Jonathan Edwards' Early Philosophical Notes." *Journal of the History of Ideas* 25 (1968).

Heimert, Alan. "The Wilderness and the Frontier." *The New England Quarterly* 36, no. 3 (September 1953).

Helm, Paul. "John Locke and Jonathan Edwards, A. Reconsideration." *Journal of the History of Philosophy* 7 (1969).

Hill, Christopher. "Science in Seventeenth-Century England." *The BBC Listener,* 7 June 1962.

Holbrook, Clyde A. "Jonathan Edwards on Self-Identity and Original Sin." *The Eighteenth Century* 25, no. 1 (1984).

Pierce, David C. "Jonathan Edwards and the 'New Sense' of Glory." *The New England Quarterly* 40 (1968).

Raven, Charles E. "Living Things in the Frame of Nature." *The BBC Listener,* 13 August 1959.

Rupp, George. "The 'Idealism' of Jonathan Edwards." *The Harvard Theological Review* 62 (1964).

"Some Old Letters Relating to Early Stockbridge, 1749–1754." Reprint from *Scribner's Magazine* (February 1895).

Stein, Stephen J. "The Quest for the Spiritual Sense: The Biblical Hermeneutics of Jonathan Edwards." *Harvard Theological Review* 70 (January–April 1977): 109 ff.

Wasserman, Earl R. "Nature Moralized: The Divine Analogy in the Eighteenth Century." *ELH, A Journal of English Literary History,* no. 20. (March 1953)

Williams, David R. "This Consciousness That Is Aware—Emily Dickinson in the Wilderness of the Mind." *Soundings* 66, no. 3 (Fall 1983).

Index

Addison, Joseph: on moral progress, 119

Affections, 37; and the heart, 63; and love, 104; proportion as test of, 49, 104, 105; and self-love, private, 111, 114–16

Ambiguities: bodies in Heaven, 87–88; brain and sense organs ideas, 61–64; duality of mind and nature, 60; knowledge of atoms, 66–68; nature both physical and idea, 32, 55–62, 71; perception as cause, 57; real existence and God, 43–44; reality dependent on mind, 59; science and Bible, 81–82; two-world theory, 92–93

Analogy: Butler on, 50–51; creation filled with, 49, 51, 92–93; metaphysical basis of, 101, 103

Anderson, Ruth Mastin, 7

Anderson, Wallace E.: on Berkeley, 56; on Edwards's interest in physics, 38; on Edwards's lack of minute observation, 24

Angels: creation of, 38, 39; status of, 38, 39

Ashley, Rev. Jonathan, 9

Atoms: attraction and interrelation of, 45–46, 103; chaos and ordering of, 38; knowledge of, 66–68

Attraction, 45; as consent, 103, 108; in nature, 47

Augustine, 122

Bartlett, Phebe, 36; Edwards's observation of, 36

Baxter, Richard: his criticism of Royal Society, 37

Beauty: and consent and knowledge, 112; principles of, 37, 48, 60; secondary and spiritual, 117–18; in Trinity, 49; of world, 34, 35

Being in general. *See* God

Benevolence: and God, 107–8; and moral sense, 114–16; to others, 106–8

Berkeley, George: Edwards and Berkeley on materialism, 41, 43; empiricism and substance, 41; on nature and morality, 100; relation of Edwards's to Berkeley's ideas, 56, 58, 59, 62

Bible: unity of, 94; writing of, 85

Billings, Edward, 9

Bisterfield, John Henry: on relation of all things, 46

Body and mind: body as medium of spirit and Satan, 60; brain and sense organs, 61–64; distinction between, 31–32, 60, 65; effects of, each on other, 65–66

Boston, 17

Boyle, Robert, 37

Bréhier, Émile: on Berkeley and Edwards, 56

Bulwer, John: on toads and spiders, 26

Burnet, Thomas, 15; on ruin of world, 39, 100

Calvinism, 95, 124–25

Causation, theories of, 57–58

Chain of being, 38, 39, 44, 118, 121

Clark, Ricarda, 11

Connecticut Valley, 9, 10; Dwight's description of, 20; isolation of, 21;